ZEN

tennis

ZEN
tennis

PAUL MUTIMER

EASTERN WISDOM FOR WESTERN SPORT

HarperCollins*Publishers*

HarperCollins*Publishers*

First published in Australia in 1997
by HarperCollins*Publishers* Pty Limited
ACN 009 913 517
A member of the HarperCollins*Publishers* (Australia) Pty Limited Group

Copyright © Paul Mutimer, 1997

HarperCollins*Publishers*
25 Ryde Road, Pymble, Sydney NSW 2073, Australia
31 View Road, Glenfield, Auckland 10, New Zealand
77–85 Fulham Palace Road, London W6 8JB, United Kingdom
Hazelton Lanes, 55 Avenue Road, Suite 2900, Toronto, Ontario M5R 3L2
and 1995 Markham Road, Scarborough, Ontario M1B 5M8, Canada
10 East 53rd Street, New York NY 10032, USA

The National Library of Australia Cataloguing-in-Publication data:

Mutimer, Paul, 1955-
    Zen tennis : eastern wisdom for western sport.
    ISBN 0 7322 5726 3.
    1. Tennis. 2. Tennis - Psychological aspects.
    3. Philosophy, Oriental. I. Title.
796.342

Typeset in Bembo
Printed in Australia by Griffin Paperbacks

9 8 7 6 5 4 3 2 1
99 98 97

ABOUT THE AUTHOR

Paul Mutimer is forty years old, married with two children. He lives in Hampton, Victoria, Australia. While he is already a successful psychologist and tennis coach, Paul's interest in dreams, imagination and the use of meditation have led him to develop his theory of successful motivation, the result of which is Zen Tennis.

Paul has written numerous articles for magazines and newspapers on coaching tennis and his unique Zen approach. He teaches people to use their sport to gain awareness of their inner responses and shows them how to use this knowledge to enrich all areas of their life.

"In my work as a psychologist I realized that I, along with many of my clients, held a belief that success was something other, more talented people had. I felt it was important to challenge this idea rather than succumb to it. By using the Zen Tennis principles of 'being in the moment' without judgment, we are freed up enough to have a go."

Paul Mutimer, 1996

For Maureen, Kate and Henry

With thanks to:
Peter Wines
Alison Leydin
Mimi Sabina
Neville Gall
Ross Duncanson
Anne Mutimer
Michael Coates
Maureen and John Watson
Peter Johnston
Christine Battersby
Australian Tennis magazine
Men's ATP Tour

Special thanks go to:
Pete Crofts
Lerys Byrnes
Evonne Goolagong Cawley and Roger Cawley
Richard Tsui-Po, Golden Lion Academy
Ben Ellwood
Mahani Mackie

Thanks also to:
Denise Barnes, Greg Brandenburgh,
Robin Freeman and Carolyn Leslie
of HarperCollins*Publishers*

CONTENTS

FOREWORD

During my pro tennis career there have been many occasions where I suddenly began to play incredibly well. I would feel an absolute "oneness" with the ball, my racket and my opponent's movement around the court. During the final of the 1974 US Open against Billie Jean King, I played the entire match in that wondrous state which players would describe as being in the "zone". The record books show that I lost 7-5 in the final set but my memories to this day of that final have nothing to do with the result – indeed I wrote later: "Quite simply, our tennis had transcended the scoreboard. Our rallies seemed endless and yet, after another exchange of impossible returns, I felt goose bumps rise on my flesh as the crowd roared its approval."

I felt like I was floating in cruise control, as if other energies had taken over. Reflexes were at work but my body had given itself over to a perfect oneness of mind, body and spirit. I was dancing to an inner rhythm with everything.

To have this feeling for an entire match was rare. I believe it only happened two other times in my career and you'll be pleased to know I won both of those! However, over time it would happen for periods during a match usually when I was behind and had decided to "go for it". Nothing could intrude on me at those moments. Hitting the ball would be effortless and I would be superaware of the racket strings brushing against the ball to the point that I *was* the strings and the ball. Sounds wonderful, does it not, and believe me to achieve that state within the high pressure confines of championship tennis was particularly satisfying.

As you go on to read Paul's book you will realise that it is just as enjoyable a state to attain in everyday life. Thanks in large part to my Aboriginal heritage, and certainly due to what I have learned from the teachings of my Aboriginal elders, this very natural experience of contentment of self continues today in my life and is no less a pleasurable, if annoyingly intermittent, occurrence. It is quite definitely something to strive for and as you read *Zen Tennis* you may recognise that you have had this wonderful experience yourself. If not, you may learn how to let it happen.

Evonne Goolagong Cawley

INTRODUCTION

THE DISCOVERY OF ZEN TENNIS

"I don't care if I die, I'm going to win this point!" In any tight tennis match this thought would enter my head, spurring me on to greater heights. I might not have had the most ability but my bloody-mindedness would never be in question. Any mistake or loss of point would sharpen my resolve.

It came as a surprise when as an invincible fifteen-year-old I started spending time in bed with a crook back. At that time I had no concept of any link between my physical condition and my attitudes. It was easier to live with the naive belief that it was just a physical problem that would disappear in time. This was not the case. By seventeen I was visiting orthopaedic specialists, physiotherapists and masseurs.

I felt a little lost and overwhelmed in this medical world. I hadn't known that there were so many different choices of treatment. I shunted myself around between the various groups but no-one had a magic wand. The general consensus was that the muscles in my lower back were tightening up and putting strain down my legs. I was prescribed a series of exercises and some muscle relaxants. Needless to say this didn't work quickly enough for me and my commitment started to waver.

Confronted with an uncertain diagnosis and the constant frustration of not being able to practice, I faced what I thought at the time was my only choice: to play and suffer or not play at all. Seeing things in such a black-and-white manner led me to stop playing tennis and look for the cause of or a cure for my condition.

Having tried many conventional methods of physical treatment I decided it was now time to see if I could benefit by exploring the powers and effects of the mind.

Maybe it was synchronicity that at this moment a few friends had just learnt to meditate. Their excitement and enthusiasm was contagious. I had to learn. "When's the next meeting?" The following night I found myself listening to a Transcendental Meditation teacher expounding the limitless virtues of meditation. I'm not sure that I really understood much of what she was saying, but a part of me felt as if I had found the answer to all my problems. In my idealistic zeal I thought it was only a matter of closing my eyes a few times and the mysteries of the universe would be revealed.

After all, if I couldn't be a tennis champion the promise of enlightenment didn't seem a bad consolation prize. Meditation became my new obsession. My mantra replaced the tennis ball.

The time that had previously been reserved for tennis was now given to this new pursuit. It was central to my life. I read books on Eastern mysticism, Zen and the martial arts. I enrolled in long meditation courses designed to speed up my journey. I felt that I had stumbled upon a great gift.

Regardless of the circumstances, and often to the bewilderment and amusement of many people, I would excuse myself when it was time to meditate. Over the years I meditated on trains, on the back of trucks, in bathrooms, toilets, just about anywhere that you could sit and close your eyes. Meditation could not be missed!

For the next seven years I religiously closed my eyes and waited, watched and experienced.

I was so absorbed in this inner world that it wasn't until I received a phone call from a friend that I had an opportunity to realize how I'd changed.

THE FULL CIRCLE

"Would you be interested in being involved in tennis again? I have a client who's looking for someone who knows a bit about the game to work at his tennis center".

"All right," I said, "after all, I'm looking for some work and it might be fun to be involved in tennis again."

The next week I found myself working on the reception desk, surrounded by the sights and sounds of tennis. How the wheel turns!

It wasn't too many days before my curiosity got the better of me. My session on the desk had finished and I was about to head home. A group of players had arrived for their game but were one short.

"Could someone make up the four?" There was no-one about except me.

"Would you play?" they asked.

"I haven't played for a long time. I'll probably be pretty hopeless."

"Don't worry, so are we," they said.

As I walked onto the court I wondered what to expect. My back didn't seem much of a worry any more but then again I hadn't been playing tennis.

I began a little tentatively but was pleased with the fact that I was hitting reasonably. Just being on a tennis court seemed like I was moving back to another lifetime. This hit was the first of a few gentle light-hearted games that were to follow over the next weeks.

I guess it didn't come as a great surprise when after six months I was asked by the owners whether I would be interested in helping out with some coaching. They had seen me playing and knew that I had played quite a deal in the past. "Why not give it a try?" I thought. So I began.

Up until now my return to hitting had been very calm and controlled. I hadn't been placed under any pressure, but as a coach, I knew that I would have clients who would want good, competitive games. Would I be able to meet the challenge?

I didn't have long to find out. One of my clients suggested we play a competitive set. "Sure," I said.

We began and my adrenalin began to flow and with it my old thinking surfaced. "I don't care if I die, I'm going to win!" Roused into action, I battled and fought my way through the game. The next day I could hardly walk. What had happened?

I hadn't felt this way in years. Was I back to square one? Did I have to give the game away? Maybe, I thought, but one of the useful things I'd learnt through meditation was to observe myself. And so the next day as I hobbled out onto the court I decided to "watch" myself and see how I played.

It wasn't long before I experienced the connection

between my thoughts and attitudes and their effects on my body and game.

I experienced how my self-doubt tightened my body. I felt the strain of thinking "I don't care if I die, I'm going to win." And I became aware of another choice. I didn't have to either give up tennis or suffer. Instead of tightening up in order to win, I could take a risk and relax. This seemed a simple solution. As I approached the next point, I could hear the doubts flooding in.

"Would this relaxed approach work?"

"Would I embarrass myself?"

"Would I lose? What then?"

I could feel myself wanting to take back control. I noticed my hand tightening its grip on the racket. I could feel the tension produced by fear and self-doubt. Was I the only person who felt this way? Could I relax and let go?

It was out of this inner challenge that Zen Tennis surfaced.

I began to realize how much of my thinking was influenced by the result. How my self-image was threatened by the prospect of losing. I noticed my mind was always entering the future. Would I win? Would I lose? I saw that tennis was revealing much of the way I thought and felt.

Along the way I began to discover that I could play a match and not end up in pain. I found by hitting the ball in a relaxed, flowing style I could experience a sense of wellbeing. I realized that my imagination could become a positive part of my tennis and that I could feel creative on the court and enjoy hitting a ball purely for the sense of relaxation it created.

Gradually I began to see a strong connection between Eastern philosophies and their application to tennis. The *satori* experience, of being fully in the moment, found its expression in watching the ball. The flowing gentle movements of Tai Chi became possible in tennis. The need for the balanced approach of Hard and Soft techniques of Kung Fu became obvious. The apparently distinct worlds of tennis and meditation started to come together. I began to see a bigger picture operating in my life that drew these seemingly different worlds together.

THE PHILOSOPHY BEHIND THIS BOOK

In writing this book I have tried to develop a philosophy behind the sport of tennis, a philosophy that takes into account the physical, mental and emotional aspects of the game. In doing so I have drawn on Japanese Zen, Chinese martial arts, Indian meditation and Western psychology.

The exercises in the book are a mixture of on-court and off-court processes designed to increase your self-awareness and improve your tennis. In keeping with the Zen tradition of story telling I've included some of my fables and poems to highlight and reinforce certain viewpoints. These are valuable methods of teaching because, instead of spelling out messages, they invite the reader to think about the issues themselves.

A personal reason for the inclusion of the poems and fables is that, for me, they are signs that I am loosening up enough to express my creativity. I see them as a spin-off from my approach to tennis becoming less rigid. This is in keeping with my belief that changes in one aspect of my life pervade all others.

By taking this total approach, I believe we can gain full value from the time we allot to our game, regardless of our standard. However, the most important benefit to be drawn from this is the development of a set of attitudes and qualities that we can take into all areas of our lives.

- I've learnt how to challenge my conditioned thinking and focus more clearly on the here and now rather than be lost in the past.

- I've rediscovered my creativity, imagination and the pure enjoyment of play and have begun to see how all aspects of my life are interconnected.

In this way sport should not be seen as something separate from work and relationships, but as a reflection of and mechanism for developing them. In this way our sport remains alive, creative and spontaneous.

The journey's end

Why begin
When there is no start
Why begin
When there is no end

The journey
Is to realize

The start
Is the end
The statement
Is better
Than the question

Begin!

BALANCE

PLAYING IN THE "ZONE"

Most people who have played tennis have, at some time, come off the court and recalled a great shot. Whether it was a serve, backhand or volley it was memorable, because it was beyond what they thought was possible for them. It gave them a glimpse of another realm. After the match they may speak, in almost reverent tones, of the backhand they hit down the line.

"I was running flat out, my opponent had hit a deep shot into the backhand corner and moved into the net. Then something strange happened. It was as if time stood still. I imagined hitting the ball down the line. I knew I could do it. Whack! With only inches to aim for, I hit it. It zoomed past his outstretched racket for a winner. I was as surprised as he was."

On a good day you may have played a number of these shots, and just occasionally you may play a match like this. It is as if you enter a "space" or "zone" where fear or doubt can't penetrate. In normal conversation we speak of these times as "having a purple patch" or "having the ball on a string."

P EAK EXPERIENCE

In psychological terms such an experience is described as a "peak experience." It is not only the property of sportspeople, but is the term used to describe the times when a person feels inspired. It is the experience of being lifted beyond your normal performance to something greater. The experience holds special qualities where the time seems to stand still, where the mind is free from distraction and where there is an unshakable sense of inner calm. Everything in that moment appears perfect.

SATORI

In the Zen tradition, the term *satori* is used to describe a moment or time of enlightenment. The experience connects us closely to our true nature, or Self, which is unclouded by the past or future. Although this may sound very mystical, it is really the experience of being natural. *Satori* can be the outcome of Zen practices and occurs when the practitioner is fully focused in the moment. It is the natural harmony of mind, body and emotions flowing together. It is a state that many people stumble across, attain for a moment, lose, and spend the rest of their life seeking. It is from these states of mind that works of inspiration are created, whether it be the memorable tennis match, the great painting or a musical masterpiece.

Once we have a glimpse of *satori* it can become a lure in itself. The experience creates a sense of magic in life that can transform the mundane into something special. It can equate with the experience of being in love, and color all aspects of life.

Satori

Tingling all over
Lightness of being
Movement dance-like
As if in a dream

A tip of the finger
Guiding the flight
Unerring precision
Effort so slight

Mind and body
Performing as one
No past, no future
To overcome

A faint smile on the lips
The hint of surprise
Imagination in action
In front of the eyes

This moment of truth
Containing all
No shadows cast
Between player and ball

RESULTS AND SATORI

In writing a book entitled *Zen Tennis*, I sometimes feel uneasy. It is as though I am being observed inwardly by a smiling face. I even get the feeling it might be an elderly monk from a by-gone era. He humorously notes my attempts to write about a way of playing tennis as if there is a formula to follow. Even the act of putting this many words down on paper is to confront the Zen saying:

> Those who know do not speak
> Those who speak do not know.

Zen has been described as a pathless path where nothing needs to be done in order to attain enlightenment. Enlightenment is said to exist at all times. We just need to realize it. It is something that happens to us rather than a result of things we consciously do. Ideally the experience of *satori* is totally satisfying and not attached to results. This viewpoint is made clear in the well-known Zen saying:

> Before enlightenment,
> Chop wood,
> Fetch water.

> After enlightenment,
> Chop wood,
> Fetch water.

Having said this, the Zen tradition still places great emphasis on disciplines and techniques. Some of these, which will be discussed later in greater detail, include long periods of meditation called *Zazen*, *kinhin* (walking meditation), study of *koans* and chanting. With many of these practices, great attention is paid to detail and ritual. How one leaves and enters the meditation hall, eats, sits, stands up and walks are all guided by various routines. So, even though the destination is ever present, we may need some help to realize it.

In the case of tennis:

- What is the destination?

- Is it becoming a Wimbledon champion?

- Is it uncovering the fact that there is a Wimbledon Champion inside us who is clouded by misconceptions?

- Or, is it the arrival of an attitude to the time spent playing?

- Is it a valuing of every moment?

- Is the tennis equivalent of the above Zen saying:

Before Wimbledon
Serve ball,
Hit forehand.

After Wimbledon
Serve ball,
Hit forehand?

The only answer that seems reasonable is that it can be all of these things. In the Zen tradition there is usually not one right answer. It may be simply a case of discovering what is right for you, at any particular moment. If your reason for playing is to be a champion, so be it, or if it is just to play for the experience that's fine as well. Every moment adds to the sense of who your real self is.

THE *SATORI* SHEET

It would be valuable to complete the *satori* sheet on page 19 to help you recognize that you may have already experienced this state. While we don't want to live in or dwell on the past, many of us become so preoccupied with our everyday commitments that it is easy to forget some of the more inspirational moments of our life. Recalling these experiences can be of great value.

By taking the time to review these moments we may find that important aspects of our life have been forgotten without our noticing. We may have stopped taking time out to exercise, we may have stopped meditating, and so on. Restoring these activities can lead to a renewed zest for life.

When it comes to tennis, if you have lost confidence in your game, it is possible you have become focused on some negative aspects. At these times it is easy to become flat and lose the enjoyment of playing. Replaying and reminding yourself of these uplifting times may help to rid you of your doubts and renew your faith in yourself. As long as you use the memory as a reminder of what you are capable of, rather than a comparison with how you are playing at the moment, this exercise can be very beneficial.

When filling out this sheet, it's important to remember that *satori* experiences don't have to be linked to great achievements. Often they can occur at very simple natural moments. I would consider that I experienced some very special moments hitting tennis balls early on spring mornings. The air was crisp and invigorating, my body relaxed and alert and I felt a great sense of wellbeing.

THE SATORI SHEET

• Recall and describe a time when you played your best tennis.
Where were you?
Who were you playing?
Did you do anything different to prepare?
Did you do something consciouslyto create it?

• What was the experience like?
Were you relaxed?
How were you breathing?
How was your sense of time?
Did you see the ball clearly?
What was your concentration like?

• Did you notice what was happening around you?

• Did the feeling last after the match?

• Did you have the experience often?

• Could you consciously repeat it?

• Have you had similar experiences while doing something else?

JOHN NEWCOMBE'S
SATORI EXPERIENCE

The following is John Newcombe's description of an experience of *satori*. It also gives some valuable insights into how he achieved this.

I have managed to achieve a satori or "peak experience" several times, which in my layman's terminology I called "putting myself in the zone." The most notable and rewarding for me personally was the 1970 Wimbledon final against Ken Rosewall.

As a nine-year-old I had listened on the radio to the 1953 Davis Cup finals in Melbourne between Australia and the US with the teenage whiz kids Rosewall and Hoad representing Australia. In 1954 they played again in Sydney and this time I sat in the stands with my dad and dreamed of the day I would be good enough to be on court.

Now, here I was in a Wimbledon final against Rosewall. I expected the crowd to be with Ken as he was older and they felt it may be his last chance to win.

Following a close first set to Ken I won the next two comfortably and at 3–1 up in the fourth I appeared to be cruising to my second Wimbledon singles title. The crowd had other ideas as they began cheering every mistake of mine and cheering wildly for every winner Ken made.

I allowed emotions to get the better of me and became full of anger, frustration and negative energy as Ken ran out five games to level at two sets all.

On the change of ends I had a serious talk with myself that went something like this: How badly do you want to win? Yes, I want to win very badly! Okay, then you need to purge yourself of all negative energy, and go onto the court with a vision only of a tennis ball and a player at the other end of the court. Everything else must become irrelevant, such as the umpire, linespeople, ballboys, crowd, friends, family and the fact it is a Wimbledon final.

I actually felt myself go inside my body and blow out all the negative feelings. I clearly remember a point at 15–30 on my first service game. I served a fault and Ken was standing in trying to apply the pressure on my second serve. Without ever really debating it I calmly aced him on the centre line. From that moment on the match was mine as I felt I knew what Ken was going to do before he hit the ball, and I ran out the set 6–1.

Afterwards, as I reflected back on the match, I was very proud of how I had been able to put myself into a zone within the short space of a sixty-second changeover, when my body and mind had been overcome with negativity. It was a great lesson that you can overcome the monsters such as fear, anxiety, anger and frustration.

I have been able to repeat this experience but I will never again be under the same pressure as in the cauldron of Centre Court Wimbledon.

While I will analyze this experience in more detail later in the book, I believe a few important points need to be mentioned now. John Newcombe's account describes his capacity to refocus his attention back to the here and now, by purging himself of his negative energy. As a result he gains a sense of calmness and knowing which stays with him throughout the rest of the match. Finally he gains a belief in his ability to overcome his inner monsters. These points are all consistent with the earlier description of *satori*.

Earlier I mentioned that during the experience of *satori* the mind is free of the distracting influence of thoughts. However, once the experience is glimpsed, certain questions, like the following, inevitably arise in our minds.

- Is this experience repeatable?

- Is it a random event left to chance?

- Can I do anything that encourages this to happen more frequently?

- Was it luck, just a destined moment or is it a matter of desire?

- Is this state of mind the domain of the champion only?

These natural questions provide the mental direction to gain a greater understanding of these times. Answering them may take you on many interesting journeys. You may meet people or read books in order to find pieces of the jigsaw or you may be lucky enough to have the experience repeat itself with little effort. As long as you don't become too interested in intellectually *understanding* the experience at the expense of "*having* the experience" these questions are valuable.

I wrote the fable, "The porcelain saxophone" while wrestling with the issues involved in enjoyment, expectations and results. It gives a glimpse of *satori*, its loss and its rediscovery.

The porcelain saxophone

Even as a young child he loved music. He would pick up any instrument and play with it for hours. As he grew older he chose to specialize in the saxophone because he found its soulful notes expressed most closely how he felt.

It wasn't long before people gathered around to listen to the beautiful sounds he produced. His face shone with joy as he played.

To repay him for the pleasure he gave them the people of his town commissioned a special gift. They hired an artisan to make a unique porcelain hand-painted saxophone. This fragile instrument was not only beautiful to look at but also had a magical tone. The young musician loved it.

He grew more famous and wherever he played audiences were spellbound by his music. After each performance they would all comment on the beauty of this precious instrument and its remarkable sound. Time passed and the young man started to enjoy the attention he gained from performing but he also secretly began to wonder whether the audience would love his concerts if he didn't have this fine musical instrument. He began to doubt his ability and worry about his performances.

Then one night as he carefully unwrapped his saxophone his worst fear happened. His hand slipped and the instrument dropped to the floor, shattering into pieces.

He couldn't perform without it. The audience would be disappointed. He couldn't go on.

The young man stopped playing altogether. At first he tried to interest himself in other activities but his heart wasn't in them. He became restless and wanted to get away from the memories and the people who kept asking him when he was going to play again. He started traveling and wandered far from home.

Years passed. He had many experiences and time dulled the memory of his playing days but, still unfulfilled, he decided to return home. It was night time when he arrived at his village and as he had nowhere to stay, he headed for an old cobbled laneway where he knew he could take shelter.

Once there, he started to clear a place to lay out his blankets. As he pushed some rubbish aside he heard the sound of metal scraping on the stones. Looking closely he saw, to his surprise, a battered old saxophone. As he cleaned it, he realized that it was dented and had surely passed its best days. Could it even play a note? Picking it up, he noticed how comfortable it felt in his hands. It was the first time he had touched an instrument since that terrible moment in his past. He lifted it to his lips.

Expecting nothing, he began to play. Tentatively at first. He felt like that young child of a lifetime ago, until he forgot himself, lost in the soulful, stirring sound. Meanwhile his enchanting music stopped passers-by and drew the attention of curious residents. Some opened windows, others wandered outside to listen.

With eyes closed and face glowing he continued.

THE CONCEPT OF
YIN AND YANG

Two protagonists of tennis who fought many battles in the 1980s were John McEnroe and Bjorn Borg. An intriguing aspect of their matches was the contrast in styles and temperaments. McEnroe displayed the passionate, "let it all hang out" approach while Borg always appeared cool and in control. McEnroe's game was full of flair and creativity whereas Borg's was unnervingly consistent. What they did have in common was a great desire to compete, along with tremendous concentration when it counted. Both were great tennis players. Based on the example of these two players it is obvious that there is no one "right" personality for tennis.

Even though we all have a predisposition to a certain temperament, there are times when it would be either necessary or useful to be able to draw on other familiar aspects of our personality. I wonder if there were times when it would have helped either Borg or McEnroe to be a little like the other. It's hard to imagine Borg firing up and doing his block or McEnroe playing a tight match calmly, but there were probably times when it would have been beneficial. Being adaptable enough to draw on an opposite aspect of your own personality provides flexibility in handling different circumstances. Being aware of these opposites and using them appropriately leads to a greater sense of balance.

In Chinese philosophy, the concept of balance is described in terms of Yin and Yang. Yin and Yang are seen as complementary opposites, dependent on each other for definition. Nothing is absolutely one or the other. Each section of the symbol contains a small contrasting circle illustrating the fact that within Yin there is some Yang and vice versa.

Some obvious examples of these opposites are:

YIN	YANG
feminine	masculine
soft	hard
night	day
receptive	active
inward	outward

The emphasis on balance is an integral aspect of Chinese life. For example if someone is sick, their treatment often revolves around diagnosing imbalances relating to an over-, or under-emphasis on Yin or Yang.

A simple example of how this could occur is through a person's approach to exercise. Exercise is a Yang element and rest is a Yin element. Too much exercise leaves a person tired and reduces their ability to cope physically, mentally and emotionally. In xtreme cases it can lead to disabilities such as dehydration and reduced functioning of the auto-immune system. On the other hand, too little exercise can result in physical problems such as poor circulation and loss of strength and flexibility. Finding the right balance is the key to maximizing good health.

●

TIGER, CRANE OR DRAGON?

Another area where this concept is highlighted strongly is in the martial arts system of Kung Fu. In the Wu Shu system, balance is achieved by having a blending of Yin (soft) and Yang (hard) movements, whereas other types of martial arts may concentrate more on either Yin or Yang force. Karate is largely a Yang art because of its emphasis on strength and power. A hard, powerful punch is countered by a strong, forceful block. Martial arts such as Aikido rely upon the Yin aspect by redirecting or evading the force of an opponent's attack.

The principles of Kung Fu were derived from the observation of different animals in their natural setting. It is thought that in the thirteenth century, Pai Yu-feng, a Wu Shu expert, choreographed the famous Shaolin system named after five animals.

The Shaolin system is a combination of breathing techniques used in association with physical martial arts, which mimics the movements and spirit of selected animals. The choreography is intended to combine the movements of various animals into a set routine, which displays Yin and Yang in various forms. When one changes from a Crane technique to a Tiger technique it is necessary to show the change in execution from supple and restrained to hard and aggressive. This allows the practitioner to more accurately mimic the animal's movements and display the spirit or personality of that particular animal.

The choreography also allows Yin and Yang to be displayed by alternating between high (Yang) and low (Yin) techniques, hard (Yang) and soft (Yin) techniques and by changing the execution of movements between fast (Yang) and slow (Yin). These same principles can be applied to tennis where shots could be varied between hard and soft, and short (Yang) and long (Yin).

The discipline and commitment necessary to master the movements were seen as an essential aspect of each monk's development. The training consisted largely of breathing, stretching and meditation exercises combined with a strictly controlled diet. The rigorous training forced the monks to go beyond self-imposed limitations and enabled them to gain insights into their true nature. This acquiring of a new viewpoint and the freeing from illusory concepts of the self can be seen as *satori* experiences.

The animals that follow the system are:

TIGER: strength, courage, spirit

LEOPARD: stealth, speed, aggression

CRANE: balance, grace, calm, concentration

SNAKE: timing, flexibility, agility

Of the animals mentioned above, the Crane and Snake represent the Yin, and the Tiger and Leopard represent the Yang. The animals are classified as either Yin or Yang according to their temperament and behavior. The Snake and Crane are both rather placid (Yin) animals that would prefer to flee (Yin) rather than fight (Yang). The Crane is renowned for its long life, which is attributed to its powerful Yin force. Similarly, the Snake uses its Yin power to maintain life during hibernation in winter. The Tiger and Leopard display their Yang natures by being aggressive and physically powerful.

A fifth animal, which is said to combine the Yin and the Yang, is the mythological Dragon. This supernatural beast is considered by many Chinese to be a mystical and godly animal and is included in this system as an ideal that can be constantly strived for. It is said that the Dragon can quickly fluctuate between weightlessness (Yin) and being extremely heavy (Yang). It is equally at home in the sky, on the ground or in the water. Its abilities are consciously determined according to its current situation.

THE RELEVANCE OF YIN
AND YANG AND THE
ANIMALS TO TENNIS

To develop a complete and balanced game it is necessary to become aware of your strengths and weaknesses. It is not enough to have a great forehand if your backhand is weak.

In the same way it is not always to your advantage to hit a ball aggressively or, conversely, to play only "touch" shots. You need the versatility to be able to choose the type of game that is appropriate for the situation and your opponent. To be able to draw on the necessary shot or mental approach means being comfortable with both the Yin and the Yang of tennis.

What would some Yin and Yang qualities of tennis be?

YIN	YANG
Crane, Snake	Tiger, Leopard
Can wait and hit the the ball late	Hits the ball on the rise
Plays with touch and finesse	Hits the ball powerfully

Movements flow with little effort	Movements short and sharp with physical strength
Works a point with patience	Gets rallies over quickly
Responds to opponent	Dictates play
Enjoys slow surface	Enjoys quick surface

Earlier when I described the meaning of Yin and Yang I said that nothing is totally Yin or Yang. There is always some aspect of one in the other. This list of players is based on their game falling more predominantly into one category than the other.

YIN	YANG
Alex Corretja	Jim Courier
Martina Hingis	Steffi Graf
Conchita Martinez	Aranxta Sanchez Vaccario
Mark Woodforde	Mary Pierce
Evonne Cawley	Thomas Muster
John McEnroe	Monica Seles
Stefan Edberg	Andre Agassi
	Pete Sampras

In making the list I found it more difficult to fit contemporary players into the Yin category. This is due possibly to the power that is generated by modern-day rackets. In the past players such as Ilie Nastase and Ken Rosewall displayed more of the style that emphasized finesse and touch.

If we continue to follow the analogy with the Chinese system then the ideal player, the Dragon, would have a blending of the following qualities: aggression, determination, persistence (Yang) along with balance, flow and agility (Yin). They would be able to choose and adapt their play as required. This player would be one whose game could be adapted to both fast and slow surfaces and would put them in the running to win a Grand Slam. As very few players have won it, it indicates how difficult it is to master all aspects of tennis. In recent years in women's tennis, Steffi Graf has gone on to win one, while Monica Seles went very close in 1992. I wonder whether they would see themselves as complete players, or Dragons.

In men's tennis, Jim Courier, Andre Agassi and Pete Sampras have all gone close to winning the four major tournaments in different years.

The player whose game I believe is the most complete and therefore closest to the ideal of the Dragon is Pete Sampras. While there is no doubting his courage, spirit or power (all Yang qualities), he does demonstrate strong Yin traits. His movement around the court between points is slow and loping, when volleying his hands are relaxed and contain a great deal of touch and his recent displays of emotion on the court could all be described as Yin characteristics.

Even though our personalities may predispose us to be more naturally Yin or Yang in our approach, to develop a "total" game we need to practice both.

Let's say two opponents are Snakes who enjoy moving the ball around the court. After a time it becomes obvious one has greater touch than the other. What are the other player's options? If they become stuck in their Snake nature then they will probably go for greater angles and look for even greater touch. Their game will be pushed to an extreme. However, if they step out of the moment of battle to assess the situation they might decide to change their approach and experiment with using some Tiger/Leopard attributes. This might be the time to attack more and introduce greater power.

If you are having difficulty getting the feel of playing in a different manner then you could try using your imagination and let yourself "become" one of the animals from that style.

It's often too late to start this experimentation during a match. It's important to allot some of your practice time to hitting the ball in different ways. If you're someone who always waits for the ball, see what happens if you take it on the rise. Conversely, if you have no patience in a rally, challenge yourself to keep the ball in play and maneuver your opponent around the court before hitting the winner.

If you are having difficulty getting the feel of playing a different way then you could try using your imagination and let yourself become a Tiger on the court.

Allow yourself to feel a Tiger's strength and courage, notice your strong decisive moments, prowl with a Leopard's stealth, imagine your opponent is your prey. Or, conversely, picture your own fluid movements. Become the Crane, with your effortless flowing style, or glide like a Snake around the court.

The only way

Many years ago there were two monasteries nestled into the base of either side of a mountain. One group of monks followed the path of the Yin techniques while the other the Yang. There was much debate between them as to which style was superior. Finally it was decided that the champion of each monastery would play off to determine once and for all which was the better approach.

The day arrived for the match. A large crowd had gathered. Two very fine athletes opposed each other. One was a tall, sinewy figure who moved gracefully and played all his strokes effortlessly. The other was a solid, muscular type who aggressively prowled the court and hit each shot as if it were his last.

The match began. The ball was served and then returned back into play. The Tiger powerfully hit the next shot, deep into the corner, the crowd rose to applaud, but the Crane moved effortlessly into position and with great touch played an immaculate drop shot just over the net. This must certainly be a winner. Not to be outdone, the Tiger raced into the net and picked it up. Shot after shot was punched or counter-punched into play. Who would weaken? After all this was still the first point. The audience were spell-bound as both players continued to trade shots. Hours passed and still no score.

The players were exhausted. Then it happened. As one hit the ball high into the air, both collapsed. The crowd held *their breath. Depending where it landed there would be a result. The ball was just above the net when to the disbelief of all watching, it split in two. Both halves fell to the ground, one part landing on one side of the court and the other part landing on the other.*

The crowd was stunned. In front of their eyes lay the two players, unable to move with half the ball on either side.

In silence, each player was picked up by his fellow monks and carried back to their own monastery, still uncertain as to which style was the best.

EXTENDING THE
KUNG FU SYSTEM

Although the Kung Fu system revolves around the movements of the Crane, Snake, Tiger, Leopard and Dragon, you may feel that there is another animal that gives you a sense of strength, power or grace. Experiment with this idea. The following list may provide you with a few ideas.

ELEPHANT: huge strength, stability and balance

EAGLE: keen eyesight and power

TREE-DWELLING MONKEY: flexibility

LION: regality, pride, strength, authority

KANGAROO: ability to jump great distances

MONARCH BUTTERFLY: ability to travel great distances, endurance, stamina, lightness

CHEETAH: great speed

HUNTING DOG: ability to pace itself, follow until prey is exhausted, then attack

Many ancient cultures actually used dances and rituals to help get in touch with the qualities attributed to certain animals. The American Indians were so convinced that they even took on the names of certain beasts. Although you may initially feel a little self-conscious, first decide which animal has the qualities or traits you either need or admire. Think of ones that would benefit your game. Is it the strength and stability of the Elephant? Is it the keen eyesight of the Eagle? Once you've done this, spend a few minutes imagining the chosen animal using these attributes. Next see yourself endowed with these qualities. How would it feel to move with the speed of the Cheetah or move around the court with the lightness of the Butterfly. Who could forget Muhammad Ali's famous warcry, "Float like a butterfly, Sting like a bee," with which he taunted his opponents. As he spoke the words he often lightly danced while darting out punches. The secret to gaining benefit from this sort of exercise is to allow yourself to let go enough to imagine and feel.

VISUALIZATION: THE USE OF IMAGERY IN TENNIS

When I suggest to various clients or pupils that they picture a certain style of play, or imagine achieving a specific goal, they often reply that they can't do it. They feel sure that they don't "see" anything with their eyes closed. However, in most cases, after a little prompting they realize that is not the case. Their mental images are forming so naturally or quickly that they don't recognize it.

Visualization involves the use of imagination from all the senses to create images and effects within the mind and body. If you feel uncertain of your own ability to visualize then try this little exercise.

Think of a room that you go into regularly. It might be your bedroom, your office or another room. Recall some objects in the room.

- What color are they?

- What size or shape?

- Do you associate certain aromas with this room?

- Is it generally warm or cold?

- Is there much light in this room?

Start by using familiar situations to gain confidence in your capacity to form mental images. If you have been able to successfully answer these questions it is almost certain that you were "seeing" these images in your mind.

INVOLVE ALL THE SENSES

Try and utilize all of your senses when creating the image in your mind. An example of this could be:

You see yourself on a tennis court that you play on regularly. It's a warm, sunny day and you feel the gentle warmth on your skin. You are moving smoothly around the court, your legs feel strong and your breathing is smooth and rhythmical. You hear the sound of your feet sliding on the court surface and the effortless impact of the ball on your racket. With minimal tightening of the hand the shot you've imagined happens before your eyes.

IS SOMETHING REALLY HAPPENING?

Invariably when using mental imagery when working with a client they'll ask, "This all sounds really nice but am I just kidding myself? Is something really happening? Is my body responding to these images?"

These are good questions and are well answered by Tom Kubistant in his book *Performing Your Best*.

The effectiveness of mental rehearsal is based upon two physiological facts. First ... the basal parts of the brain and the central nervous system could not differentiate between something that was actually happening versus that which was being vividly visualized. The higher parts of the brain make this differentiation. Second ... when one is vividly visualizing a moment, all those nerves that fire the muscles used in the movement are being electrically stimulated at a lower, yet significant magnitude.

To those doubters among us, it is reassuring to hear that our bodies respond on a physiological level to the images formed in our mind. Something is really happening! It's not a matter of blind faith.

How is this useful for your tennis? If we think of our body as a car, then mental imagery is part of the tuning that prepares it to move. The engine is switched on but the car is stationary. It's ready to move. In the same way, by applying mental imagery to your tennis, you are firing the necessary cylinders or muscle fibers that are to be used in your movement. By clearing the connections you're ready for action.

TELEVISION IMAGERY

During a time when there is major television coverage of tennis the games of many of my pupils (especially children) seem to go through change. Their style seems to pick up the mannerisms and approach of whichever player ignites their imagination. This is often done unconsciously and it can be a bit of fun guessing who's their favorite player. This mimicking was obvious when Bjorn Borg inspired a crop of

Swedes to play baseline tennis with his trademark double-handed backhand.

Once we realize that we can be influenced by the images we see on the television screen (this is the basis of any advertising campaign) we can put this time to good use. Select a player whose game excites your imagination. You may admire their mental approach, it might be the power with which they hit the ball or you may like their style. Spend some time watching them play. You don't have to concentrate hard on what they are doing. Just sit back, relax and soak up their play.

The next time you're on the court allow yourself to copy the odd mannerism of their game. Although you don't want to end up a clone of that player, and lose your individual approach, you may find that you gain a little of the quality you admired.

On a slightly different note: I've often been tempted to put a video together of top players making bad mistakes. This would be useful to show players who are perfectionists and give themselves a hard time over every mistake.

NEGATIVE IMAGERY AT PLAY ON THE COURT

During coaching sessions it has become obvious how many players reinforce and recall their mistakes. On many occasions I have been working on a particular shot with someone and feel that we are making good progress. They may have hit nine good shots in a row. Then they make a mistake. The next moment is full of expletives, tantrums and the declaration: "I can't play such and such a shot." This belief and the accompanying image of failure are the ones that become strengthened. Remember to try to focus on the positive aspects of your training. A word of warning: be careful which images you focus your mind on!

DREAM EXERCISE

As a means of encouraging your imagination try the following exercise.

• Spend a few minutes relaxing.

Monitor your breathing.

Listen to its rhythm.

Hear its sound.

Allow your analytical mind and beliefs to be put aside.

Allow yourself to be a little unrealistic.

Try not to stop your imagination before it starts.

• Now drift back into your childhood. Take a little time. Ask yourself if you can recall your earliest dream.

What was it that you imagined?

Was it a sporting dream? See if you can get the feel of it.

• Allow yourself to experience the excitement and enthusiasm involved in your imagination.

• Give yourself some time. Be prepared to let your mind mull over this for some time. Don't worry if nothing comes to mind initially. Be patient and be willing to try it a few times.

• If a past memory came to mind ask yourself the following questions:

Did you achieve your dream?

If not, what happened?

Was it just too unrealistic?

Did someone tell you it couldn't
be done?

Did some experience bring about a sense of self-doubt?

What beliefs did that create for you?

Can you remember the disappointment?

Did you dream a different dream?

Did you stop imagining?

Are you dreaming now?

What are your beliefs now? Reinforce the value of dreaming and this memory by writing it down somewhere. Perhaps draw a very simple image that reminds you of it. Place this where you will see it regularly so that you benefit from the visual reinforcement.

BELIEF

THE THREE ESSENTIAL ELEMENTS OF ZEN

It is said in sporting circles that ninety per cent of the game is played above the shoulders. When two players of equal physical ability compete it often comes down to who has the strongest psychological make-up that determines the result. Many sports people put themselves into a winning position only to lose due to their own doubts. Thoughts such as "I'm not good enough" or "Surely I couldn't beat so and so" enter their mind and generate images and feelings that undermine performance.

This type of thinking is the main challenge to experiencing *satori*. The sense of flow that epitomizes the experience is interrupted and our true ability or potential is not displayed. Performing to a level lower than we know we are capable of is perhaps the greatest cause of frustration in our sport.

- Where do these negative messages originate?

- What can be done to change them?

In answering these questions I have drawn on three essential elements to the practice of Zen. These are said to be great doubt, great faith and great determination. All three are interconnected and either reinforce or influence each other. Change one and we automatically affect the others.

Great doubt

It may sound unusual to have this listed as a positive aspect of practice in any field, until we examine what it is we are doubting.

The doubt here refers to the conditioned beliefs that we hold to be true about ourselves, our life and, in this case, our tennis. Being able to doubt the validity of statements that limit our perception of ourselves and our game is a tremendous asset. When our self-talk says "You're not good enough," or "You'll never amount to much," doubt suddenly becomes valuable.

Great doubt asks the questions:

- Who says you are no good?

- Why do you believe this statement?

- How do you know it's true?

- Are you sure?

- Why couldn't you be successful?

In exploring these questions we often have to admit to ourselves that we don't know why we think that way. Maybe it is true that "we're not good enough" but have we really assessed it for ourselves? Great doubt challenges us to put our preconceptions aside and honestly reappraise our beliefs. This process can take time and in the short term leave us feeling confused. However, this temporary discomfort can lead to a much deeper sense of our true nature because our beliefs become a result of our own thinking. During this period of challenge it is useful to have great faith.

It is essential to become aware of our inner communication because we may be sabotaging ourselves without knowing it. Our opinions, beliefs or judgments are influenced by our upbringing and early conditioning and our continuing experiences. These opinions or judgments may be empowering or limiting.

This form of "doubting" leads to an honest assessment of our own truth, not a passive acceptance of someone else's opinion.

GREAT FAITH

To enter the uncertain world of doubt it is valuable to have faith in other possibilities. We need to be able to imagine more for ourselves than our limiting messages suggest.

Faith is the voice inside that reassures us that all is fine, that it is all right to have uncertainty in our lives, especially if it leads to a greater knowledge of our self. Faith encourages inquiry but teaches us to stop grasping at answers. Faith gives us the strength to wait until we do know. The reward of faith is trust: trust in ourselves and trust in life's uncanny ability to direct the right people, situations and circumstances to us.

At times when our faith is wavering from the tension produced by great doubt it is useful to call on our will and great determination.

GREAT DETERMINATION

For someone like myself whose faith wavers, great determination is essential. If doubt starts the journey and faith reassures us along the way, then determination carries us across the line. Great determination strengthens our resolve to find the answer to our questioning. It provides the passion and will to change.

Great determination supports the saying that most breakthroughs in human endeavor require "ninety per cent perspiration and ten per cent inspiration."

THE WINDOW
OF CHANGE

Great doubt springs from the mind, great faith leads to the heart and great determination provides the desire and will to finish the journey. This combination of elements provides a model for describing change: a window for looking past our conditioned selves and gaining a new insight into our psyche.

Moments of change in our life can be viewed through the lens of the "three greats." An example of how this interaction works can be gleaned from John Newcombe's *satori* experience.(I have analyzed John Newcombe's experience. He did not fill this out himself.)

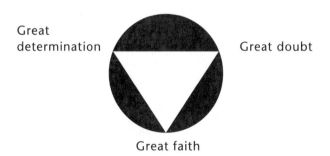

Great
determination   Great doubt

Great faith

The window of change

JOHN NEWCOMBE'S WINDOW OF CHANGE: 1970 WIMBLEDON FINAL

Great doubt

- *Conditioned belief: crowd has control over him (and therefore, the result). Belief results in feelings such as frustration, anger, etc.*

- *Challenges this belief.*

- *Method: self-talk: "… you need to purge yourself of all negative energy."*

Great faith

- *Needed faith that another possibility existed. Needed to doubt the truth of his conditioned belief.*

- *Faith in the possibility he could control himself in these circumstances.*

Great determination

- *Provided by the will and desire to achieve his goal. Displayed in his self-talk: "How badly do you want to win? Yes, I want to win very badly! OK then."*

- *Result: Blew out all negative feelings.*

New insight

- *Able to control his own feelings.*

- *Can overcome monsters such as fear, anxiety and frustration.*

In looking over this process it is clear how John Newcombe initially allowed the crowd to affect his feelings and threaten his goal of winning Wimbledon. When he challenged himself through some strong self-talk he was able to transform his negative feelings and achieve his desired result. Importantly he gained the insight into the fact that he could control the monsters such as fear, anxiety, anger and frustration.

In the next section we will look a little more closely at our self-talk and our possible responses to it.

Why not?

Why not you?
Why not me?
Success belongs to somebody

Why not you?
Why not me?
Is it a matter of
Luck, desire or destiny?

Bounce of the ball
Roll of the die
Will and emotion
Is where the path lies

Why not you?
Why not me?
Perhaps it's
Luck, desire
And destiny

Why not?

THE INTERNAL DIALOG

Yoda: Luke. You must unlearn what you've learned.
Luke: I can't, it's too big …
Yoda: That is why you fail.

(*From* The Empire Strikes Back)

Much of the way we communicate with ourselves is learnt from our parents or family members. This process begins very early in our lives so that our drives, values and morals are in place before we even realize it. It is as if we look at life through a pair of colored glasses that highlight certain facts and edit out others. This can take the form of dialog we have within ourselves. Sport is a tremendous vehicle for becoming aware of this inner conversation.

Earlier we looked at how we can use great doubt as a means of challenging these conditioned beliefs. It questions our inner dialog in order to discern which inner messages are beneficial. For instance, you might tell yourself, "If you try hard enough you can do anything you want," or "Never give in." You may have self-doubts in the form of "I'm not good enough" or "I'll never amount to anything." Some of these messages passing through our minds are loud, as though they are being blasted through a speaker, while others play quietly in the background, almost unnoticed.

When we are under the pressure of competition this internal dialog, some of which is unconscious, is highlighted and brought to the surface. If the messages are positive and useful then we will run with them. However, any "inner messages" we are not comfortable with will have to be worked through and modified.

What can bring them to our attention is an uncomfortable experience, like losing a match we were expected to win. On close reflection we realize that as the match hung in the balance our inner dialog was "You're no good if you lose."

What are some of the possible responses to this scenario?

1. I feel lousy but become determined to train harder, so I don't lose.

2. I feel lousy, fear losing and begin to lose motivation and interest in my sport.

3. I feel lousy and examine my thinking to see if it needs to be changed.

Let's look at these three potential responses to losing a match and the discovery of the accompanying inner dialog, "You're no good if you lose."

1. If we use the spur of the disappointment of losing, and the fear of the judgment of hearing "You are no good," as a motivational force to improve our game, then we are

gaining some benefit from the loss. However, we may still have, buried inside us, a tension that surfaces and undermines our game when a match is close. We may sense the voice of judgment looming and try too hard, or tighten up under the inner pressure.

2. In the second scenario the enjoyment and pleasure is taken from our game and we become dispirited and give up. We may feel that this is all we can do; however, at some point similar challenges might present themselves under different circumstances. We might be just delaying the inevitable confrontation.

3. This is where great doubting can come into play. It asks the questions:
   – Who says this is true?
   – Where did this statement come from?
   – Why should you believe this statement?

   This leads to the process described earlier where the three "greats" operate, creating a window of change where a new perspective can be gained.

One reason why this thinking can be so entrenched and difficult to change is due to the fact that it is learnt at such an early age. It has been there so long it feels part of us. It's difficult to recall a time when it wasn't there. We learn to respond to situations in a certain way for so long that our behavior becomes automatic.

Let's continue to use the above situation as our example because the issue of winning and losing is central to the sporting situation.

Inner conversation: "If I lose I'm no good."

In examining this statement clearly we need to consider:

- Who says this is true?
- Where did it come from?
- On what do you base an acceptance of "If I lose I'm no good"?
- Has anyone said this was the case?

As small children we absorb the feelings and thinking of those around us. We soon learn what sort of behavior brings what responses. This then reinforces in our minds what to do. After a while, in certain situations we act and think in such an automatic way that we no longer consider whether there are any alternatives.

This conditioned response is obvious in the animal kingdom. In India when an elephant is young, one end of a rope is tied to its leg and the other to a strong tree. The young elephant tries to break free and can't. It feels the resistance to its efforts and eventually associates the feeling of the rope at its leg with being unable to move. After a time of reinforcing this condition, the rope can be lighter and a smaller tree can be used. Even though the elephant by this time could easily break the rope or snap the tree, it recognizes the feeling of the tug on the leg and doesn't move.

Luckily as humans we are not confined to live with our conditioning. At the time of learning these responses we may have felt as though there was little choice, but now as an adult, things can be different. By challenging our beliefs it is only a matter of time before we change.

Be patient with yourself. The emotional aspect of these beliefs can take time to let go.

AFFIRMATIONS AND THE MENTAL DRIVE

If you have become aware of an attitude that needs some adjusting then it's up to you to put the work in. Sometimes mental shifts occur almost instantaneously while at other times hours of rehearsal are necessary. The development of mental skills in tennis works in the same way as physical ones. Approach them as though it were another ground stroke, say the "mental drive."

One aspect of this mental drive is the use of affirmations. These are positive statements that we use to reinforce certain messages that we need to hear. By repeating them to ourselves, either internally or externally, we challenge any ideas to the contrary that lie in our subconscious. Repetition will force the negative thinking to the surface and eventually out of our system. For instance, if you have a belief, "I am no good at sport," buried deep inside then to create an affirmation, "I am good at sport," will push the negative message to the surface to be reviewed. You may find that the old belief wasn't true after all.

If you have become aware of the need to work on a new belief what do you do? You have become aware that you need to reinforce a new belief. You're clear as to what the old one was, so how do we develop and utilize the new one to gain maximum benefit?

- Begin by writing the new belief. It could be:
  - I am relaxed under pressure
  - I am in control of myself
  - I am a valuable person
  - I am focused in the "here and now"
  - I am an excellent tennis player
  - I have a great backhand

- When writing it put it in the present tense, as if you already possess this attitude. For example, "I am confident" or "I relax under pressure."

- Write it on a card and place it where you will regularly see it. In much the same way advertising reinforces messages by constantly displaying them on the screen, we can absorb the message just by having it around us. Take a card with your message onto the tennis court with you. Have it in your bag so that you can read it at the change of ends. This can help to focus your mind. You could even try writing your new belief in poem form. I wrote "Fire dreaming" when wrestling with the idea that I could be successful.

Fire dreaming

●

Fire in the belly
Fire in the mind
Fuels the Imagination
Ignites the Dreamer's Soul

At times
A blazing Sun
Alive in victory,
At others
A spark within the ashes
Of defeat and injury

Whether
Standing on the dais
For all the World
To see,
Or
Watching on
Feeling lost
Alone and empty

One thing
To be sure of
Once the vision is alight
The flame will never die
The Dream beats
Forever in the hearts
Of you and I

Fire in the belly
Fire in the mind
Fuels the Imagination
Ignites the Dreamer's Soul

THE USE OF DREAMS AND IMAGINATION

What if you slept,
and what if in your sleep you dreamed,
and what if in your dream you went to heaven
and there you plucked a strange and beautiful flower
and what if when you awoke you had
the flower in your hand?
Oh, what then?

Samuel Taylor Coleridge

Tennis, like all areas of achievement or self-expression, has repetitious, disciplined aspects. Many hours need to be spent repeating technical aspects of strokes in order to produce them automatically. It requires dedication and commitment to reach a high level of proficiency.

Many people set goals in order to succeed. They usually map out logical, coherent steps to achieve the desired result. However, if the goal they've set doesn't excite them, if it doesn't stimulate their imagination, then achieving it will be a mechanical soul-less exercise. Others start out enthusiastic but for various reasons lose the initial enjoyment. In tennis, the stress of competing at an early age has dampened the interest of many young players. (In order to prevent burn-out occurring, the Women's tour recently ruled that no player could become a full-time professional until they were sixteen years old.)

Why is it that some people find the constant striving an obstacle to their progress while others appear to enjoy it? I believe this is where it is important to have the ability to dream and imagine and to stay in touch with the excitement they create.

To instill passion, enthusiasm, creativity and spontaneity into our goal setting we need to "dream" and imagine ourselves achieving and experiencing these future results. By combining the analytical mind with the imaginative process we are calling into play both hemispheres of the brain and therefore gain a total approach.

THE CAPACITY OF CHILDREN TO IMAGINE

We only have to observe children at play to realize how active their imaginations are. The ability to be creative and involved in the imaginary world seems to be an inherent aspect of childhood.

The capacity of children to imagine was brought home strongly to me when I was asked by one of my clients to coach his five-year-old son. This was a new challenge for me as I had coached mainly adults for the previous ten years. Not wanting to burden the boy with technical instruction I was trying to make the lesson fun, but I realized after a while that he had lost concentration and wasn't watching the ball. I suggested to him that when the ball bounced he could yell out "Yes." He did this happily to begin with, probably enjoying the fact that an adult had asked him to call out something rather than try and quieten him.

After a few extremely loud yeses I thought it might be fun if he made up something himself to call out. I asked him whether he would like to do that. "Sure," he said, "I've already thought of something." Without asking him what he had in mind I prepared to hit the next ball. What was he going to scream? I only hoped he wasn't going to swear at the top of his lungs.

I hit the ball and waited expectantly for the bounce. I couldn't believe it when "I'm a great tennis player" was screamed back on top note. It was an unashamed expression of how he saw himself and an extremely powerful affirmation. There was no doubt in his mind at that moment that he imagined himself as a great tennis player. Such an image of himself created a great faith in himself.

How many adults would entertain this image, see themselves this way and allow themselves to express it openly? Even those who had allowed this thought, might dismiss it very quickly with another like,

"Don't be ridiculous!" or "Be realistic!" Our doubts wouldn't allow us the luxury of these images.

While we don't want to deceive ourselves regarding our ability it is equally important to allow ourselves to entertain the possibilities we imagine.

Why adults lose the ability to dream

Do we stop dreaming because memories of failing to achieve our early goals are painful and stop us taking the risk to try again? Imagination and dreams magnify and highlight our feelings and so, inherent in the use of imagination is the possibility of great euphoria and deep disappointment.

By letting our minds drift into the future and imagining something bigger and better for ourselves we simultaneously dredge our past experiences. If we allow ourselves to entertain the image of being a great tennis player then we will need to confront the fears and doubt that this image may disturb. These are usually the result of past experiences and memories and hold a strong negative emotional charge.

To dream successfully into the future we need to confront our past, let go of the emotional baggage associated with it and replace the unwanted images

with new ones. In doing this we ultimately achieve
psychological freedom.

THE MIND CREATES
THE MAP

To stay in touch with our dreams it is useful to have
definite, achievable steps and sign-posts along the way.
Remember the dream provides the emotional fuel for
the journey, the mind creates the map.

When setting these goals it is useful to break them
down into manageable pieces. I've done this in the
Dream Map (see page 73). Firstly, dream your big
goal; don't put the brakes on. Allow your imagination
free rein. If something comes to mind put it down
and worry about the reality of it later.

If you're working on your tennis dreams an obvious
example of a "big dream" would be winning
Wimbledon. For most of us, however, a big dream may
be winning our club championships. This may seem
like Wimbledon to us. For the sake of the exercise
we'll use winning the club championship as our dream
and follow through the necessary steps as an example.

Having decided on your dream draw a symbol or
image that represents it. Try and make this fun. When
I suggest doing this, many people cringe and say they
can't draw. Remember to let your inner creative child
out to play. The image could be something obvious

like a trophy or you could represent this dream by an abstract symbol. If you are struggling to come up with an idea, you might find something appropriate in a magazine. Once you've decided on an image, then put it somewhere you'll see it regularly. It might be near the bathroom mirror, on the fridge or even the dashboard of your car. Seeing it regularly will keep you connected to your dream.

Now imagine some of the benefits of achieving this. Feel the excitement that these changes will bring!

Before you continue, imagine the benefits of achieving it.

- What would it mean?

- Would it mean you've conquered many fears and doubts?

- Would it lead to greater confidence in all areas of your life?

- Would it mean that you had gained a level of fitness that you'd never attained previously?

- Would it be an opportunity to demonstrate a deeper sense of commitment to a goal?

Next, give yourself a sign-post that indicates you are on your way. Imagine or think of something that you could achieve in one month that would indicate that you are well and truly on the right path.

Working our way backwards, using our example of winning the club championships, what would be a sign in one year's time that you were on your way to achieving your dream? Could it be in this year's club championships that you get to a further stage than before? Could it be beating a player that you've never beaten? We are assuming that your dream/goal will take more than one year to achieve but you might get there more quickly than you expect. If this happens obviously you would need to re-dream your goal.

What could your six-month sign-post be? If you play competitive tennis already you might be performing better. If you haven't played in a team before this would be an excellent goal to aim for.

Your one-month sign may be achieving a breakthrough in your technical expertise. You may improve your second serve or get that topspin backhand you've always dreamt of. You may challenge yourself to get more comfortable at the net.

Now to the nitty gritty of getting to your dream!

ACTION STEPS!

This is an extremely important part of the process. What can you do this week that will contribute towards your monthly goal being achieved? Make these steps achievable. If you create something too difficult you could lose confidence or momentum.

It is important to date, sign and have someone witness this sheet. Making a contract with yourself reinforces your commitment to your goals. When choosing someone to witness these goals and action steps see if you can find someone who is interested in following the process through for at least six months. What sort of person do you need? Someone who acts like a watchdog? Someone who encourages and supports you?

When I first started writing, I set up a regular meeting with a friend who challenged me to keep up the action steps I'd set. Having a definite time each week gave me a structure to work with. Get used to ticking off the steps as you go. Keep it handy so that you remind yourself of your goals. Obviously as you are setting weekly action steps you will need to spend time on it on a weekly basis. Keep your old sheets in a folder so as to be able to look back over your progress. At the end of each month reset your monthly goal and check whether you feel you are on target to meet your six-monthly one. If not modify it.

Although to arrive successfully at your goals is a good feeling in itself, it may be useful, and act as an incentive, to reward yourself for achieving your steps along the way.

This contract with yourself can serve to reinforce your goals. By taking the time and effort to write it down and have someone witness it, you will start to give the dream a shape or form. What was previously a nice idea has moved from your mind into the outer world

The aspect of reward is optional. While achieving the goals in themselves may be reward enough for some people, others might motivate themselves by deciding that meeting certain targets is deserving of some special recognition. This can still be related to the main goals set. For instance the reward may be a new tennis racket, a tennis lesson or even a tennis retreat or weekend.

A DREAM MAP

Area of Dream

Dream

Draw a symbol to represent it

Imagine some of the benefits of achieving this Dream
List some:
1
2
3

One month

Six months

Twelve months

Action steps
1
2
3

Date
Signed
Witness
Evaluation:

Reward (if necessary):

DREAMS DON'T DIE

When setting sporting goals we may reach an age where we realistically have to face the fact that we may not be a Wimbledon champion. However, we can still choose dreams and goals that challenge the same processes. We may do it in a sporting area or we may set ourselves the dream of achieving excellence in a completely different area. Inevitably we discover that the same attitudes and thoughts that prevented us from reaching our sporting goal are unearthed again. It's never too late to be involved in the experience of dreaming.

When I had the idea of writing this book, I knew that it would take a great deal of persistence, firstly to actually write it and secondly to get the go-ahead from a publisher. So to keep my eye on the ball I decided to get a cover made up for the book. One that would excite me. Luckily through a chance meeting it happened. Once I got the image I wanted I had it framed. I placed it on my office wall so that each day I reinforced the fact that this was going to happen. Two years down the track it did.

However, as the publisher had a different image and goal in mind, the cover I'd visualized needed to change. Who can argue with a publisher? But, the important factor was that the process of keeping in touch with the dream helped it to become a reality.

Voyage

Imagination
Letting go
Untie the moorings
Go with the flow

Voyage begins
Destination where?
Alone at the helm
Of excitement and fear

Tide, current, wind
Nature's friends and foe
Stars and moon
Bearings to go

Whether lost at sea
Or land ho!
Riding each wave
On a high or a low

Close eyes to make room
Somewhere to go
Imagination's double edge
Is what makes it so.

BODY

In sport, the experience of *satori* is often accompanied by the physical feeling of relaxation. Movements are described as fluid, flowing, controlled and natural.

If this is the case, then to be able to monitor and regulate the tension in your body when you play is essential. The exercises in this chapter are designed to create greater awareness of the state of your body and more choice in controlling it.

AWARENESS AND CONTROL

When playing sport it is easy to tighten up without realizing it. Therefore it is important to regularly check whether this is happening. To tell your body to relax is beneficial. However, it is such a general instruction that you may not experience any tangible results. This is where it is useful to utilize the area of your body making contact with the racket: your hand.

Think of the times you have played a "good shot," that is it went in for a winner, and looked good to the observer. Yet you did not feel good about it yourself. Often the reason is that you don't feel connected to the shot. You may find out, if you closely monitor your play, that there is some tension either in your arm, shoulder or hand that is blocking you from sensing the ball hitting your racket.

When the ball hits your racket it vibrates and feeling this is important. It is generally not registered as a conscious sensation followed by the thought, "Oh there's the ball hitting my racket." However, if the grip is squeezed too tightly then you will block out all sensation and not feel connected to the shot. Hence you don't feel in control or good about the shot.

MONITORING TENSION

Start this body awareness training in your practice sessions. Have someone hit a ball easily to you so that you can begin to monitor the tension at the grip without too much pressure. Notice the tension at various stages of the swing and the rally. Observe what your hand is doing at end of the backswing, when you connect with the ball, and while the ball is down the other end.

Experiment with the moment of hitting the ball by using differing degrees of tension in the hand. If you are unsure whether you are tense or not, provide a contrast for yourself by tightening your hand on the racket and then releasing it. This exercise often leads you to be able to find the correct tension. By keeping some awareness on the grip you could stop your game getting "out of hand."

Try and develop the habit of consciously relaxing your grip on the racket after each shot so that you short-circuit the possibility of gradually accumulating tension. With practice you will begin to recognize more quickly the times that you start to react to some thought or feeling by gripping your racket tightly.

Once you have gained this awareness, and experience the results of tightening up, you will probably be motivated to change. At the very least you now have a choice. You can either continue to hit with tension or see what happens if you relax your grip. Don't expect yourself to "let go" every time. It may take time to gain the confidence to trust this process. Don't judge yourself if you do tighten up. Use the information and feedback to help next time. Be patient.

At times you may feel that even though your hand is relaxed you are still tense. This is possible. I've included other exercises in this chapter to help deal with this. However, getting feedback on your hand tension is an excellent start to gaining awareness and some control of your body.

❧

S H O W   A N D   T E L L

Once a player becomes aware of whether or not they are tense, they can start to assess their errors in terms of whether they were flowing or whether they had become too rigid. If they have the realization that a certain mistake was caused by bodily tension the usual response is to give themselves the mental instruction "relax and hit through the ball." This in itself is a useful piece of advice. However, this instruction can be taken one step further and that is by actually taking a practice swing exactly like the one you are suggesting.

When taking this swing (obviously between points), it will register more strongly in your memory if it can be done with your full attention on the sensation. Therefore when called upon it will more likely resemble the type of stroke you want. Even try doing this with your eyes closed so that you cut out unnecessary stimuli. Learning to register and trust this feeling is extremely beneficial. Instead of approaching the ball with a lot of mental clutter we can just allow a particular feeling to come out.

In the Zen tradition the teacher often demonstrates a skill which the disciple observes and attempts to repeat. Mistakes are seen as a necessary aspect of learning and verbal teaching is kept to a minimum.

I can recall a tennis lesson where the person I was coaching was a perfectionist. After every mistake she asked, "What did I do wrong?" At first I suggested to her that she was doing well and that she just relax and swing at the ball. But she couldn't contain herself and it wasn't long before she inquired, "What happened then?"

I took a breath, resisting the urge to give her more information and said, "The ball went out of the lines."

"Is that it? Is this what I'm paying you for?" she said.

"Yes," I replied.

She looked at me a little annoyed until a faint smile formed as she realized that I was resisting the urge to clutter her mind.

An internal reference point

Another important aspect of body awareness is to feel that the dimensions of the court are part of you rather than experiencing them as something external. What I mean by this is that many players, for example, hit the ball short all the time, as if the baseline was somehow controlling their behavior. It is as if it were saying "Don't hit the ball near me or else." So we continue to hit the ball short. If we take the risk of hitting the ball long at times, we will get an internal reference point that tells us what it feels like to hit the ball deep. When we have that feeling inside we can refer to it for direction rather than be intimidated by an external element. It is necessary to have hit the ball long to have the experience and knowledge of what that feels like.

ARE YOU REALLY LEAVING THE OFFICE BEHIND?

In the business world there is a great deal of pressure to win and not make mistakes. People are pushing themselves all the time. Their lives often become imbued with an all-pervading sense of urgency that builds up over the years until their bodies become tense under that relentless pressure.

Many business people turn to tennis as a means of releasing tension and having a different focus. However, when they get on the court they can behave the same as they do in the office: driven, angry and tense. Their sport becomes an extension of the attitudes they have towards work.

This was demonstrated when I was coaching a forty-year-old businessman who had never played tennis before. For his first lesson I gave him a simple exercise — I knocked a slow ball onto his side of the court and he had to return it. He hit the ball with a reasonable stroke. I thought, "That's not too bad." But the ball landed out. He let out a terrible scream. I thought he'd pulled a muscle. I charged across to him and said, "What have you done?" With his back to me he replied, "Didn't you see the ball was out!"

It took me about a minute to respond. "You let out that scream because the shot went out?" I asked.

"Yes," he said. "What you showed me was so bloody simple and I couldn't do it."

I hit him a few more balls and he treated each one like a live hand grenade. I started to sweat. I thought, "If he's not going to have a heart attack in the next few minutes, I will." Eventually I stopped the lesson, walked over to him and said, "C'mon, let's go for a walk." As we walked I asked him how he was feeling at the moment. He replied that he was feeling tense and frustrated. "Is this what you want from your leisure time?" I asked.

Although this person's desire to play good tennis could not be questioned, what was in doubt was the value derived from being under that constant level of pressure not to make mistakes.

On a physiological level constant arousal is bad for you. We've all evolved to cope with brief periods of arousal, such as when somebody threatens us. But in the modern world a lot of adrenalin-producing stresses go on day after day. If you're in a permanent state of fight you can find yourself feeling angry or irritable much of the time. It is important to ask yourself, "Why did you want to play tennis in the first place?" Make a list of what you want out of this recreation time.

The list I made with the businessman went something like this:

1. I need some regular exercise. I sit at a desk all week.

2. Tennis is a good social game and I can play it with a few mates.

3. I need to unwind after a week of constant deadlines and challenges.

4. I need to have a bit of fun.

If one of the benefits you want from your tennis is to relax physically and mentally then it is important to learn some techniques to achieve that.

Two major areas of focus can be used to achieve a more relaxed approach to your game and to leave the office behind.

1. Learn to scan your body for any tension during your game.

    Before you serve or receive serve, do a quick scan of your body. Notice whether you are clenching your jaw, whether your shoulders feel tight and if your breathing feels restricted. If so then simply instruct yourself to drop your shoulders, relax your jaw and take a couple of deep breaths. This will help you flow a little more and reduce the strain placed on your body. As mentioned earlier, monitor how you are gripping your tennis racket. Through this method you get instant feedback about your body and state of mind.

2. Give yourself a focus that keeps your attention in the present.

During your recreation time you may find that your mind continually wanders back to the office. You may find yourself thinking about details of meetings, contracts, etc. If you realize this, then one excellent way to refocus yourself is to give yourself the challenge of watching and seeing each ball during the match. The ball can act as a psychological "circuit breaker" to break the loop of work-related thoughts.

B E N E F I T S

One company director I coached always played with his teeth clenched. This was extremely obvious when he served. He would walk up to the line to serve, take a breath, hold it, quickly go red in the face and clamp his teeth together. I wondered whether he realized he was doing this so I asked him to observe on his next serve what was happening with his jaw. "Wow," he said, "I'm sure locking that tight!" During the next serve he tried to keep it relaxed while he hit the ball. He reported that it felt a little strange at first but as he got used to it, it started to feel comfortable. What really surprised him, however, was the fact that his serve seemed to become more reliable.

Now that he was aware of this he used this moment as a checkpoint to relax his jaw and take a few breaths. One week he reported back to me on his weekly sales meeting. "I normally get wound up and eventually blow up at someone or something. However, today I noticed early in the meeting that I was clenching my jaw and holding my breath. I did the same as on the tennis court, I relaxed and took a couple of deep breaths. The meeting proceeded without a hitch. I think everyone else in the meeting became nervous, they were wondering what was wrong with me!"

To derive maximum benefit from your tennis game it is important that you leave the court feeling refreshed, both mentally and physically. This in turn, will lead to greater satisfaction and productivity back in the work-place.

Work and play

When at work
Be at work

When playing tennis
Be playing tennis

INJURIES: ACCIDENT
OR ATTITUDE?

We have all heard of talented people in sport who had great ability but were continually dogged by injuries to the point where it forced them to retire prematurely. Rather than just passively accept there is nothing that can be done to heal the problem (which may be true) I believe it is important to explore how the attitude of the player may have contributed to the injury in some way.

One of my clients had a very bad case of tennis elbow. The initial treatment was purely physical. It was a combination of physiotherapy and rest followed by an exercise program to strengthen and increase mobility in the appropriate muscles and joints.

Having done this he got the OK to return to play. Within three weeks his tennis elbow had returned. It was extremely frustrating as he was just beginning to find form and was looking forward to the club championships.

His choices seemed to be to continue playing and suffer or not play at all. Would it be worthwhile going through rehabilitation and all the work it entailed if the condition kept recurring? After all hadn't he already tried everything? When we spoke about it I suggested there was the possibility of a third choice. Was his body trying to get a message to him that he needed to look at his technique or his mental approach to the game? What could that message be?

It is possible, for instance, that he was getting too fired up, too driven, and as a result was putting too much strain on his body. This excess adrenalin and drive may result from thoughts such as "I'm not good enough" or simply from a fear of losing and what that means to his self-image. It won't be until this attitude or doubt is challenged that the body fully recovers. He might have an over-emphasis of the harder, Yang element and need to balance it. Full recovery could depend on a combination of physical therapy and a change in mental approach.

He seemed keen to explore this option and found that there were many times when his body was under unnecessary strain. Over time, by modifying his game and continuing with his exercises, he made a full recovery.

Today, perhaps more than at any other time, it is becoming accepted that the right mental approach has a bearing on recovery from disease. Sporting injuries are no exception. So next time you have an injury, as part of the rehabilitation process, take time to explore the possibility of whether the injury is your body's way of trying to tell you something about your approach to the game. It may be a case of having to accept there is nothing you can do to prevent the injury recurring or else you may be able to save yourself a great deal of "rotten luck."

FOCUS AND CONTROL

LISTEN TO YOUR FEET

One of the more neglected areas of tennis is the use of the time between points. It is very easy to rush between points without even realizing it. This is where it can be very useful to give yourself a part of the body to focus on so that you can keep this under control.

The part of the body I find most useful to focus on is the feet. Begin by listening to the sound your feet make as you walk back to position. By simply placing your attention on this sound you will begin to regulate your speed. If you feel you are rushing, experiment with consciously walking more slowly. Keep listening to your feet hit the court as you do this.

Another reason that tuning in to your feet can be useful is if you are thinking too much. If you have so many thoughts running around in your brain that you are becoming distracted or confused then by listening to the sound of your feet you are "grounding" your energy and taking the excess mental energy away.

This will result in a quiet mind that is free to concentrate on the important and appropriate elements of the game.

PROGRESSIVE RELAXATION

This technique involves taking your attention to each section of your body in order to identify where your tension is located. The first objective is to find out what is there without trying to change it. Once this has been achieved, then by tightening and letting go the various muscle groups we can bring about a greater sense of relaxation and ease.

To do this exercise it would be useful to have someone read the text for you (see page 92) rather than try and play the role of the "relaxer and relaxee." Try recording it so that you have it for future use. If it's difficult to get someone to do this, then read it onto tape for yourself. Practice reading it a few times before you record it so that you get a feel for the right times to pause. Feel free to add or delete pieces as you become more acquainted with the process.

One important point to keep in mind is that when you are listening to this tape, do not force yourself to follow the sequence. If at any stage you find your mind wandering off, let it go. When your attention returns just pick up the tape at the point it is up to. If you try and make yourself listen and stick rigidly to the tape you will create more tension than relaxation.

Now that you have your tape, or your friend, it's time to give it a try. Find a quiet place where you can lie down comfortably and not be disturbed.

RELAXATION TAPE

Close your eyes. Give yourself a few moments to adjust to the fact you are lying down and begin your relaxation.

Now become aware of your body in a general sense. Does it feel heavy or light? Does it feel tired or energetic? Are there any strong sensations? Observe them without trying to understand them or work them out.

Now observe your breathing. Is it fast or slow? Is it deep or shallow? Is it in rhythm or is it labored? Listen to the sound it makes when you breathe out. Do this for a couple of minutes. If you become aware of your mind wandering just bring your attention back to hearing your breath.

Now we will start to take our awareness through the body in a very gradual, systematic way.

Starting at your face and head, become aware of any tightness or tension around your jaw. If you find any, allow the jaw to drop open a little and relax. Check behind your eyes, cheeks, chin and scalp for any further tightness and have the idea of letting it go. Remember, relaxation often starts as an idea and later becomes a feeling or experience.

Move your attention down to your neck. Notice how it feels. If you become aware of tension then gently have the idea of relaxing it. Move your awareness down the left side of the neck, then the right. Continue through to your shoulders and slowly down your arms. Imagine that some soothing warm water is running through the muscles and gently breaking up tension.

Once you've done this, then with your right hand, slowly make a fist, hold the tension for the count of seven, then release it. Now move your attention to your left hand. Slowly make a fist with it, hold it for the count of seven, then release it.

Become aware of the movement of your chest and stomach as you breathe. Notice the speed as it moves up and down. Once you've done this, on the next three breaths allow yourself to sigh on the out breath. Imagine your breath is like the release valve on a pressure cooker. With each sigh you are freeing any build up of tension.

Move your awareness down to your lower back and hips. Observe any tightness. Imagine all the muscles relaxing and softening. Feel your body sink further into the couch or floor.

Move slowly down your right leg. From the upper thigh move to the area behind the knee. Take your attention through to the calf, the ankle, the foot and into the toes. Move your attention to your left leg. From the upper thigh move slowly down to the knee. Relax the area behind the knee. Take your attention through to the calf, ankle, foot and toes.

Having moved through all of your body, allow a little time for yourself to drift without any instruction.

At the end of this time gently bring your attention back to your breathing. Notice it without trying to change it. Observe the sounds you can hear around you. Slowly begin to move your hands and feet. Then open your eyes. Notice how your body feels. Slowly begin to move your hands and feet. There's no need to rush. Allow yourself as much time as you need. Open your eyes when you feel ready. Lie there for a while so that there is a smooth transition back into activity.

By practicing this you will become more aware of your body and where it holds tension. This will enable you to identify more quickly when you are beginning to become tense on the court, and thus be able to respond before the "horse has bolted."

CONTROLLING NERVOUSNESS

In her book, *Make the Most Of Your Best*, Dorothy Sarnoff provides a tip on how to control nerves before public presentations. She suggests tightening the muscles of your Vital Triangle. This area of the body is formed by tracing the outline of the ribs from the point at the solar plexus, down each side of the ribcage as it splays and then drawing a straight line across at the widest separation.

By exhaling and drawing the muscles back as hard as you can, you can put the brakes on any out-of-control nervousness.

If you are someone who gets overly nervous before a tennis match try practicing this before you go onto the court. It could also be useful to try at the change of ends.

MASTERS AND DISCIPLES

THE ZEN METHOD OF CHALLENGE

The Zen masters were often notorious for their methods of challenging their disciples' determination to hang on to outmoded beliefs. To help them break free from their conditioning, one technique involved giving the young monks riddles, or *koans,* to solve.

A well-known example of a *koan* is Hakuin's "What is the sound of one hand clapping?" The disciple was meant to go off and solve this conundrum.

The student is often brought to the point where he feels stupid, as though he knows nothing. In searching for the answer he realizes how much of his thinking is *conditioned* rather than *known*.

Zen masters were often severe disciplinarians who were known to give monks a whack on the shoulder for moving needlessly during meditation. The disciple had to place great trust and faith in their teacher. This "shoulder tap" was deemed to be necessary when the pupil's attention had wandered off or when they were drifting off to sleep. The student needed to believe that the master or Roshi was awakening them for their own good.

The role of the tennis coach can parallel that of the Zen master, although I'm not sure how the Zen master's discipline would work between tennis coach and pupil. Imagine asking a young tennis player to come up with an answer to "What sound does the tennis ball make while it moves in the air?" or giving him a sharp whack with a tennis racket when a mistake is made!

E L I T E   C O A C H E S :
S U R R O G A T E   P A R E N T S ?

It is interesting to note that many of the leading figures in tennis have enlisted the aid of an older adult in order to direct, encourage and steer their careers. Do the players, under the constant pressure of battle look for and replace their natural parent with a surrogate one, their coach?

PLAYER	COACH
Anna Kounikova	Nick Bollitieri
Pam Shriver	Don Candy
Stefan Edberg	Tony Pickard
Andre Agassi	Nick Bollitieri
Pat Cash	Ian Barclay

This guidance from an older "parent" is not something new to elite tennis. In the past Harry Hopman steered the careers of many young Australians (Laver, Hoad, Rosewall, et al.). His direction entailed the discipline and authority often seen as the domain of parenting. He appeared to have some of the qualities associated with Zen masters who were renowned for their fierce, tigerish personalities. Even today, Australian tennis players are still looking for direction from the "tribal elders" with Ray

Ruffels, Bob Carmichael, John Newcombe and Tony Roche still actively involved in players' lives.

ROLE OF THE COACH

The coach can provide new insights and turn up the volume on the new communication we need to hear. The crucial part of this process occurs when the new message ultimately becomes internalized and part of the pupil's inner communication. This internalization usually happens over a period of time after the pupil has heard the coach repeat the instruction many times. After a while the coach's voice becomes the pupil's. This leads to individual freedom and self-reliance, the result of a healthy and successful relationship between coach and player. The coach then fills the role of offering insight, support and motivation without strings attached.

When we take responsibility for our inner dialog we are on the way to becoming masters of our own destiny. Our beliefs have been consciously chosen and accepted. At this point we have become our own person and have inside us our own Master Coach.

MEET THE INNER COACH

While it is useful to have a coach or someone we trust to ask for advice, it is also important to be able to trust our own instincts and intuition.

By developing an inner sense or image of our own wisdom we will feel more confident in making important decisions. This imagining or visualization is designed to get you in touch with your problem-solving ability as well as further develop your ability to imagine.

Begin visualizing by spending the necessary time you need to relax. Remember any visualization exercises work better when you feel relaxed.

Earlier this century a leading psychologist, Carl Jung, coined the term "archetype." Archetypes are patterns of human development that are universal and exist in all people, in all cultures at all periods of history. They are eternal images that attract, convince and fascinate humans. Some examples are the Hero, the Witch, the King or Queen, and the one that is the focus of this exercise, the Wise Man or Woman.

VISUALIZATION EXERCISE

Imagine you are on a tennis court in the country. The court is nestled into the bottom of a mountain. Spend some time on the court hitting up. Enjoy this time. Don't make it competitive. Create very comfortable circumstances. Make it your ideal conditions. Notice how you are hitting the ball. Swing easily without forcing anything.

After you've finished playing, sit by the side of the court and check whether there is any aspect of your game you are not happy with. If you find that something is bothering you and you don't have a solution then it is time to find the Wise Old Tennis Coach.

You've heard that in a cave on the mountain-side lives a wise old coach. So you head off in search of him or her. You climb steadily up the path winding along the edge of the mountain. Every now and then pause to get a view of your surroundings. You move on and round a corner. In the distance you see the outline of a cave. You come to the entrance. You enter. Inside you find a person whom you instinctively trust and with whom you feel comfortable. You introduce yourself and inform this person of the reason for your visit. You voice your problem. Now listen carefully for their answer. Once you feel clear that you understand the message thank them and head back to the court.

If your question was specifically connected to your game and you feel like some more imaginary practice it might be useful to see yourself walk onto the court and rehearse whatever direction you've been given. If not take a little time, then open your eyes.

Now write down on a piece of paper the wise old coach's response. Depending on the question asked and the advice you received your follow-up plan can be quite different.

If your problem was about some mental aspect of your game like "How can I overcome nervousness during a match?" your plan might involve the use of affirmations or repeated visualizations. If it was a technical problem, devise a practice routine in order to make the necessary changes.

If you have a coach it might be useful to talk over the response you received to your question so that you can work together on the change.

BREATH

" MOVEMENT WITH A BEAT "

It is almost impossible to play a rhythmical shot if your breath is out of rhythm. Well, what is rhythm?

When we hear the word "rhythm" our first thoughts are often of music or dance. It is no wonder it has been described as movement with a beat. It is usually experienced in the body as a sense of ease and flow where our timing is "just right." Yet, for something sounding so natural it does seem to have an elusive quality to it. How often have we heard people say that they "just lost their rhythm" or "their rhythm just deserted them," as if they were powerless to do anything about it because it was beyond their control.

A clue to the rediscovery of our rhythm lies in its description as *movement with a beat*. Most people report that they lose their rhythm when they become tense or tired and their movements develop an element of strain. This tightens the muscles and restricts their flow of breath.

The breath becomes uneven and loses its steady rhythm. This process may happen so gradually over a period of time that it goes by unnoticed and hence the sense of its disappearing and being lost.

One key to restoring rhythm lies in the ability firstly, to notice that our breathing has been affected and secondly, to be able to do something about it. Later in this chapter I will look at specific techniques designed to gain greater awareness and control of the breath.

Breath

A quick glance
Over the shoulder
Before the mind discloses
Its secrets

Breath,
The invisible witness
Eavesdropping
Leaves its mark
On the mirror
Pointing to
Inner conversations

Fast, Slow
Deep, Shallow
Elusive, Held

Its changes
Providing clues
To what it
Heard

DANTIAN BREATHING

The use, control and awareness of breathing is of major importance in Kung Fu and the Zen disciplines. In the martial arts all techniques are initially practiced with normal breathing. However, once some technical competency is achieved the breath is directed from a place in the body called the Dantian.

The Dantian is located approximately three inches (or 7.5 centimeters) below the navel. The purpose of drawing the breath from there is to add power and strength to each strike. The breath and the strike are coordinated by drawing the breath in from the Dantian, as the fist is taken back, and then releasing breath and fist together.

The same process could be utilized on the tennis court when playing a ground stroke. To begin with, practice the following process without the ball.

Draw your racket back and at the same time, inhale your breath. Then, as you follow through, release your racket and breath together. Repeat this process until you feel your breath and racket are working together easily. Once you can comfortably coordinate the two add the ball to the process.

As you begin to hit the ball in this manner you may notice the extra power that you can generate by combining the timing of your swing with your breath. If you have been hitting forcefully through physical effort alone this method of hitting will help to reduce the strain on your body. You may notice that you have already been doing this without realizing. Just keep on doing it. If it is new to you, then like anything else you practice, over a period of time it will become an automatic part of your game.

ADVANTAGE MEDITATOR

In Eastern culture meditation is seen as a normal and essential part of life. However, as technology has enabled information and lifestyle to be exchanged rapidly around the planet, new terms such as "meditation" have become recognizable in the West.

- What is meditation?

- What are its benefits?

- What forms of meditation are there?

- Which sportspeople practice it?

To break down the mystique the word "meditation" held in the West, and the feeling that it worked only if you believed in it, meditation has been subjected to stringent scientific research. Some of the health findings during and after meditation are:

- Drop in oxygen consumption to greater levels than the deepest part of sleep

- Biochemical responses in the body the opposite to stress indicators

- Brain wave coherence

- Adaptable arousal level

- Increased reaction time

HOW IS MEDITATION PRACTICED?

One interesting approach to meditation used in the East that parallels "watching the ball" involves the use of a *mandala*. The word "mandala" means magic circle or sphere in Sanskrit, and contemplation on one is said to bring about a deep feeling of inner peace. Circles or mandalas feature in Zen paintings and represent enlightenment and the striving for human perfection. Seen in this light, a tennis ball could be used as a moving mandala and a vehicle for self-discovery.

Another form of meditation that complements the process of "watching the ball" involves the use of a *mantra*, or sound, as a means of quieting mental activity. The process is similar to watching the ball bounce except instead of using a visual object (ball) as a focus to let go of thoughts a sound (mantra) is used.

The mantra is gently repeated internally and produces a unique state where the mind is deeply rested while still remaining alert. With regular use the mind naturally maintains this experience for longer periods. The benefits of an alert restful mind are obvious to any sportsperson.

Champions such as Martina Navratilova, Billie Jean King and Gigi Fernandez have all learnt to meditate, and obtained benefits from the practice. Meditation is of benefit to players at all levels. Regardless of the standard, as we have discussed earlier, there will always be distractions, thoughts or fears to contend with and so there is always a place for a technique that helps you to relax and focus. To actually meditate before you go on the court means that you have already dealt with many of the distracting thoughts and feelings.

WHEN IS THE BEST TIME TO MEDITATE?

Ideally, try to meditate twice a day, before breakfast and dinner. Relaxing on a full stomach is a little like trying to sleep immediately after finishing the evening meal. It can be a little uncomfortable.

The other time it may be useful to meditate is if you are having trouble sleeping. If you have difficulty getting to sleep or you wake up in the night and cannot get back to sleep, then it may be useful to use meditation to help you drift off.

The most important thing to remember is that, like everything else we do, the more regular you are in your practice of meditation the better you will become. If you are only trouble-shooting difficult moments you will probably have limited success. Try getting into the habit of meditating as a preventive measure rather than as a response to acute pressure, tension or stress.

SHOULD I MEDITATE IMMEDIATELY BEFORE COMPETING?

I don't believe there is a black-and-white answer to this question. Each sportsperson approaches competition with their own particular attitudes and temperament. Some people find it necessary to be quiet and to remove themselves from others in order to maintain their composure and focus. More extroverted types may find they relax more by being in the company of others.

You may need to experiment a little to discover your ideal pre-match meditation time.

Is it important where I meditate?

If you share a house with others it is often useful to let them know that you are practicing your meditation so that there is little likelihood of being disturbed.

Although it is not essential, some people find it useful to meditate in the same place each time. Consider taking the phone off the hook or putting on the answering machine. Remember, this is *your* time. If *you* treat it as precious others will soon get the same idea.

Myths of meditation

Many people start meditation but after a period of time conclude, "I can't do it, I can't stop my mind from having thoughts!" or "I can't do it, I don't feel relaxed after it."

These statements expose two of the myths regarding meditation.

Firstly, many people consider that for meditation to be successful they must empty their mind of all thoughts. When they close their eyes and find that thoughts keep coming, much like a river keeps flowing, they decide that unfortunately they can't do it. However, if we accept that thoughts are a natural part of us, and include them in our experience of meditation, we can relax more easily. Absence of thoughts may be related to the goal of meditation but thoughts, themselves, are accepted as part of the journey.

The second common myth regarding meditation is that during or after it we will always feel relaxed and that we will walk around with a smile on our face and be perturbed by nothing. These expectations are unrealistic. In fact, when we meditate we may end up confronting many of our past beliefs that need transforming. This may lead to feelings of tension or discomfort, in the short term, as we learn to let go of the outmoded beliefs. So, even though it can be a passive activity it can also be confrontational.

Finally, you may have begun looking for a means of meditating as a response to some difficulty in your game or life. At this point you are probably anxious to get immediate results, and you may. However, with such high expectations and hopes it is easy to end up disappointed. Try to adopt an attitude of patience when you begin. It may take time to turn around long periods of stress. Try to approach the early stages as an experiment, using yourself as the test case. If you persevere, what may have started as a discipline to improve performance or alleviate pain may turn into an interesting adventure discovering more about your body, mind and emotions. You may even rediscover that child-like pleasure that comes from feeling good for no particular reason.

Next time you head off to practice ask yourself whether it would be useful to add meditation to your arsenal of shots.

KINHIN:
WALKING MEDITATION

Awareness of the breath is a fundamental aspect of Zen meditation. One Zen practice that combines movement and breath awareness is called *kinhin*. It is interspersed with *Zazen* in order to shake off the sluggishness and stiffness that can be experienced by long periods of sitting. It is usually used only for periods of five minutes at a time.

One aspect of *kinhin* is promoting awareness of the breath as you walk. While walking the breathing can be coordinated with the stepping, counted or merely just observed. This helps us to maintain some mental separation from our thoughts and feelings, and could be carried out on the tennis court while walking to position between points. This would be useful in a tennis match as it would help prevent a player from becoming carried away or overcome by the match.

THE THIRTY-SECOND MEDITATION

An extremely valuable time to gain awareness of your breathing is at the change of ends. Probably the most memorable instance of this occurred in the 1975 Wimbledon final. The late Arthur Ashe used this time to clear and refocus his mind. It obviously helped because he went on to win the final against the heavily favored Jimmy Connors.

This is an example of short meditation (remember it can be done at home or office as well as on the court).

1. Sit, close your eyes.

2. Consciously place your feet on the ground. Then relax your jaw, shoulders and hands. You could do this by slowly forming a fist with either hand, holding it for the count of five, then releasing it.

3. Now take your attention to your breath and listen to the sound of ten exhalations. Count each one. Don't jump straight up, but take a few seconds before you open your eyes and begin to move. Don't underestimate the value of this time. Remember in John Newcombe's *satori* experience how at the change of ends he "actually felt himself go inside his body

and blow out all negative feelings." By taking
this time to observe your body and breath
you may release or prevent the build up of
tension.

ZAZEN:
SITTING MEDITATION

One aspect of *Zazen*, that is Zen meditation or sitting
Zen, which is central to the practice is awareness or
observation of breathing. This can be done in different
ways and the methods are very similar to using a
mantra, as described in earlier sections.

Zazen is considered an extremely important aspect
of modern-day Zen practice. Depending on the
monastery and the time of year *Zazen* can be practiced
for the whole day to be punctuated only by meals,
chanting and some work. The idea of this meditation is
to sit without expectation of achieving any outcome
other than the realization of one's true nature. In this
quiet awareness one simply observes without judgment
the passing thoughts and feelings. In order to help
quieten the mind and give some direction to the
practice awareness can be placed on the breath itself.

The idea is not to try to force the breath into any
particular pattern or rhythm, but merely to be aware
of it. During this time thoughts, feelings and

sensations will come into our minds and at times take the attention away from the breath. This is seen as part of the process and the attention is returned to the breath when the meditator becomes aware of the fact they have "returned."

An everyday example which highlights this is when we are tired and reading a book. We may find that we have scanned halfway down a page only to find that our attention has returned and we have no idea what we have just read. During our mental wandering, our attention has been focused on a thought, feeling etc. and not absorbed in reading. It is not until our awareness returns that we realize we have been away. At this moment we usually go back and re-read the text with awareness.

Awareness of the breath can be maintained by:

1. Counting the breaths, usually up to ten.

2. Listening to the sound of the out breath.

3. Feeling the breath at the nostrils.

Another way to practice regulating your breath off the court is to use everyday situations. Even difficult or frustrating situations, such as a traffic jam, can become extremely useful practice sessions. Instead of being frustrated and losing your cool, observe your reactions and see what you can do to maintain a sense of equilibrium.

SOUND AS AN EXTENSION OF BREATHING

An extension of the release of breath is the use of various sounds. In the Wu Shu system different sounds are attributed to each animal in order to enhance different effects we may be wanting.

For example, if we wanted to play an aggressive, powerful shot we would use the sounds of the Leopard and Tiger. This would be the sound WAH. Conversely, if we were to play a "touch" shot from our fingertips then we would utilise the sounds of the Crane or Snake. These are WUP and TISS.

The use of sound is not new to tennis: we only have to recall Monica Seles' now infamous grunts (probably Tiger or Leopard) to appreciate that the use of sound at the moment of impact adds more power to each shot.

TAI CHI TENNIS

Tai Chi is an ancient Chinese system of movement, usually performed in a very slow rhythmical manner. Its balanced series of dance-like steps are designed to restore and maintain balance in the body.

The breath is brought up slowly from the Dantian (situated just below navel) and released with the body movements. By coordinating breath and body in this slow rhythmical manner, the practitioner is said to be able to feel an inner flow of energy called Chi.

A similar and useful series of movements could be practiced on the tennis court. Very few players, once they attain a reasonable level of competency, bother to perform a practice swing. If they do, it is usually done at a very quick speed with little conscious attention paid to what they are actually doing.

It would be beneficial to establish a short routine, as part of their warm up, to practice each groundstroke at a slow speed coordinating the movement with the breath. If you keep the routine simple it will allow you to monitor both your breath and the stroke production.

A possible combination of movements and approach could be:

1. Stand at base line at center point.

   Take a ready position stance and hold it for a couple of seconds. Be aware that your weight is evenly distributed. Feel the muscles in your legs. Observe in this stationary position the movement of your breath. Is it fast or slow? Is it deep or shallow? Is it in rhythm?

2. Perform forehand stroke with breath awareness.

   Now slowly take your racket back, and at the same speed and time draw your breath in from the Dantian. Once completed, begin your forward movement and follow through at the same speed as before and once again coordinating the physical movement and the breath.

3. Return to ready position and rebalance. (Repeat 1.)

4. Perform backhand stroke with breath awareness. (Use same approach as 2.)

From this point you can build a routine using service action, movement to the net and volleys. Try to create a pattern that involves the same number of steps and takes the same time to complete each time. Even though there is the danger this could be done mechanically, the discipline and ritual of keeping movements and time together should provide a great opportunity to balance and focus yourself before you start hitting a ball.

The fable, "The rainbow made of rope," highlights the great value that can be gained by maintaining awareness of the breath.

The rainbow made
of rope

By a large bay window overlooking the harbor, a young, apprentice cobbler stood daydreaming of exploring greater horizons. He was snapped out of his mental wanderings by the old bootmaker who quietly reminded him of the task at hand. He returned to his work knowing that one day he would leave.

When the day came it caught him by surprise. He was upstairs looking out the window when a Rainbow appeared on the horizon. This one was different from others. It didn't form an arc across the sky and it wasn't ethereal. This Rainbow hung from the sky and was rectangular in shape. It had substance and appeared to be made of braided ropes.

The young man was excited and knew this Rainbow was calling him. Anxious to get to it before it disappeared, he rushed off without saying goodbye to the old cobbler.

Not daring to take his eyes off the Rainbow he hurried along the cliff-top path. Such was his haste that he didn't notice that he was headed straight for some sort of force field. Now he was caught in it. It appeared to stretch in all directions and dragged him along like a powerful undertow. He started to panic. How was he going to get out of this limbo? Summoning every ounce of strength and will he dragged himself back out to the side he had entered. Completely exhausted, he looked up, as his Rainbow disappeared.

He lay there for some time until he had enough energy to return to the cobblers. On his return, the old man greeted him with warmth and understanding and shocked the young apprentice by saying, "If you remember nothing else, the next time you are in that force field, take a strong breath! The more powerful the breath the further the journey."

"How did he know what had happened? And what strange advice," thought the young man. But he doubted whether, after that fright, he would ever want to go back again.

Time passed and he settled into his job and began to enjoy the simplicity of his life.

Again, he was surprised by the reappearance of his Rainbow. He tried to resist it but the lure was too strong. This time he stopped long enough to say goodbye to the old man.

As he headed off, he kept one eye on the Rainbow and the other on the path. He wanted to be prepared this time. It wasn't long before he arrived at the force field. Approaching cautiously, he could feel the strength of its magnetic pull. One more step and he would be in. He paused, but knew he had no choice if he wanted to reach the Rainbow.

In he stepped. Again he lost his bearings and felt himself being dragged along uncontrollably. He started to panic. How could he get to the other side? Suddenly, the old man's words came to him. "Remember to breathe!" "Surely I'm already breathing," he thought, "but what have I got to lose?" Taking his attention to his breathing, he found to his surprise that *he was holding it. Consciously he took a deep slow breath in through his mouth and released it. He felt a little calmer. He repeated it and looked up to see that his breath had cleared a cylindrical tunnel in the force field. Seizing the moment, he jumped. With arms and legs flailing in all directions he slid to the other side.*

He realized now that there was something special about that ordinary old man.

Looking up he saw the Rainbow was still a fair distance away. "Surely it will disappear before I reach it!" he thought. Then he had a sudden idea. "If I could breathe myself through the force field, maybe I can breathe myself to the Rainbow. It's worth a try."

He pointed his body in the direction of Rainbow, tilted his head, took a deep slow breath in and released it.

Before he realized it, he was hurtling through space like a human rocket. Maybe this breath had been too strong! Bang! He hit the Rainbow. He almost went past it but managed to grip the ropy strands and hang on, swinging in space for a while before coming to a halt.

From this position he could see his whole world stretched before him. His home, the village and the sea. Everything was so clear from this perspective. He filled with gratitude at being able to free himself from the force field and have this wonderful experience.

BALL

FOCUS ON THE BALL

To create the state of mind described as *satori*, we need to find a means of staying fully focused in the moment while still being relaxed. This may sound a fairly simple task, but it can be quite a difficult process to master. Why is this the case and how can awareness of the moment be developed?

Here the tennis ball becomes a useful tool. If we can focus on the ball to the exclusion of everything else then we may have a momentary glimpse of *satori*. If we know that we saw the ball bounce and we see it onto the racket after the bounce then we have been able to drop our other thoughts temporarily. The benefits of being able to do this are tremendous.

If we think of the brain as a computer and we think of awareness of the ball as the information we punch into it then the printout (forehand, backhand etc.) will depend on the quality of the information processed. If the ball is clouded by thoughts in the form of fears and doubts, then each shot is likely to be affected. The clearer our attention for the ball the more likely we are to get quality information.

GRAND PRIX TENNIS

A useful analogy that explains how easy it is to look at a ball and still not see it is that of driving the car. Let's say that when you go to work you drive the same route every day. After a few years of traveling the same way, you get to work and think to yourself, "Did I stop at those lights?" or "I suppose I must have driven past that building. I'm here intact aren't I?" Because it is such a repetitious act we use the minimum amount of attention necessary to complete our task satisfactorily.

However, if we went to bed one night and as we slept a Grand Prix race track was installed on the same route, the next day while driving to work at four times the speed we would be aware of every square inch of the drive and be able to recall it all.

This is how we should think about seeing the ball. If we want to play Grand Prix tennis we have to be aware of every instant and see every ball so as not to be overtaken by the other players.

SIX-STAGE PRACTICE PLAN FOR WATCHING THE BALL

How many times have you gone to tennis, hit up for a few minutes, had a couple of practice serves, then started playing. Five minutes later you are screaming in frustration at the mistakes you are making. What hope did you have of finding your timing, focus and rhythm? Would you be able to see the ball easily under that pressure?

It's important to remember when you are looking for the ball not to force your attention on it. If you do, you will find that you become tense and pressured. Try and allow your attention to "settle" easily onto the ball with minimum effort and minimum frustration. The exercise, the six-stage plan, which I practice regularly with my clients, is designed to create the time and structure for this to happen.

It has a feeling of completeness about it. It allows for a smooth purposeful transition of watching the ball while performing less complicated tasks, more difficult ones and back again. It allows us to gradually get into the process rather than rush it.

I believe the six-stage structure is one that warrants regular practice. This would be an ideal way to practice in the days leading up to match play and would be valuable in a shortened version to warm up the day of your match.

SIX - STAGE PLAN

1. Initially hit the ball easily backwards and forwards with a practice partner. Each time the ball bounces make a gentle inquiry as to whether or not you saw the ball bounce. You will notice that you can hit a ball without consciously remembering seeing it bounce. Don't be critical of yourself if you realize that you haven't seen the ball. Just use this information to reinforce the need to look next time. Try to be aware of the thoughts that clouded your perception. Some will be recurring ones, others will just come and go.

Use this information to reinforce the need to look next time. On more than one occasion during coaching I've asked my pupil whether they remember seeing the ball, only to find that they snap back at me, "No, I didn't!" At this stage I realize that watching the ball has become a test they feel they must pass. They have heard my question as a potential lead-in to some criticism. Try to make it an inquiry rather than an inquisition.

To facilitate this process try yelling "Yes" at the moment the ball bounces. Have fun with your practice partner to see who is the first to forget. This is a valuable concentration exercise.

Once you've practiced watching the ball in this easy manner and feel that you have it under control, it's time to increase the difficulty and move onto Stage 2.

2. The next stage, after hitting balls backwards and forwards to each other, is to increase your movement around the court.

As you pick up the tempo you may notice that it becomes more difficult to stay with the ball. When a ball is hit to the opposite side of the court it becomes tempting to charge off furiously. In doing so there is often a "blank" spot where we don't see the ball until we get close again. We may rush unnecessarily and find that we inwardly speed ourselves up and end up rushing our shot. Try and let the ball tell you how fast you need to run. Stay relaxed and keep the ball in focus as you move towards it.

3. The third stage in your practice is to start playing points, not games. It is usually a good idea to have five serves each but DON'T SCORE. Now that you are involved in playing points there will be a little more tension in your game. You won't want to hit the ball out of court and you may, despite the fact you are not scoring, try a little harder to win.

However, see if you can hold uppermost in your mind the goal of following the ball. This can be slightly harder because the above thoughts and feelings may begin to cloud it. Once you are comfortable with this move onto Stage 4.

4. Now it's time to add the extra pressure that comes from scoring. Don't actually play games yet. Make it the first to ten or twenty. Notice the extra pressure that scoring puts on the process. Does it make a difference to your ability to watch the ball now that win/lose is involved?

5. Now it's time to try playing an orthodox practice game with normal scoring. Now you are approximating match conditions. Notice the challenges that are involved.

Although this is still only practice, because you are emulating match conditions it will bring to the surface as many fears about winning and losing, not making mistakes etc., as a match can. These thoughts and feelings will challenge your watching of the ball as much as the practice.

6. Having finished your set it's important to warm down. Go back to Stage 1 and hit gently backwards and forwards again. Notice now, in contrast to playing a set, what it's like to watch the ball. Does it seem easier than at the beginning?

This systematic practice routine is beneficial because it allows you to gradually increase the pressures that come to bear on your game. Be willing to wait until you feel comfortable with one stage before you move onto the next. This time may vary from one practice session to another.

When you are comfortable with this practice routine it's time to see how you fare watching the ball in competitive matches, tournaments etc. Obviously these circumstances will increase pressure even more but at least by gradually working up to this moment you will be as prepared as possible.

If you find that your attention is constantly wandering when you are looking for the ball, try giving yourself something specific to look for. See if you can see the brand or the join on the ball. If you're hitting with topspin, see the back of the ball or notice whether the ball is spinning fast or slow.

Challenge yourself by seeing whether you can hold your attention on the ball for the whole rally. This means remembering it hitting your opponent's racket, the time it travels in the air between you, as well as the bounce at your end.

Miloslav Mecir, a former top ten player, is someone I believe focuses correctly. In an interview with Nick Place of the Melbourne *Herald*, "he [Mecir] watches the ball from the moment it is tossed into the air for a serve to the time a ballboy picks it up or it finds the net. Mecir is completely focused. You could wave a red flag behind his opponent, you could fire a gun — he is engrossed in the flying yellow missile."

DISTRACTIONS

Regardless of the level of sport you are playing there are always going to be distracting thoughts and feelings competing with the ball for your attention.

For the beginner it may be thoughts such as "I hope I don't make a fool of myself" or "I'm sure I'm going to be the worst player to ever set foot on the court." These thoughts obviously hold an emotional charge and often cloud our perception of the ball.

The advanced player will have another set of thoughts and feelings that vie for their attention. They may want to win a tournament so badly that if they get into a difficult position in a match the thought, "I think I'm going to lose," may tighten them up and interfere with their ability to focus on the ball. They might expect a certain standard of play and frustrate themselves when they play below this. Although it is possible that these thoughts and feelings sharpen a person's concentration, most players are distracted by them.

Having the ball as a focus when we are inundated with thoughts is a great asset. The reason for this is that it gives us somewhere neutral to place our attention.

ATTACHMENT

There are some common themes or attitudes that can dominate the ball. These can be different for each player. However, a few occur on a regular basis. Letting go of them can be difficult. It is as if we are "attached" to them.

So what do I mean by "attachment"? Attachment occurs when our attention becomes focused on a thought and we are unable to let it go. If this happens regularly then we have some emotional attachment or investment in the result.

ATTACHMENT: WIN OR LOSE

One common scenario that demonstrates how easy it is to hit the ball without consciously seeing it might go like this.

Jack finally maneuvered his opponent out of position by playing a powerful drive into the backhand corner. Although off balance his opponent managed to get his racket onto the ball and play a feeble return into mid-court. Jack got excited, a gleam came to his eye. There, before him, lay the entire court begging for his shot. Already he could hear the umpire calling, "Game, Set and Match!" Revved up he walloped the ball across court. There was a momentary pause. He was about to throw his clenched fist into the air when it suddenly struck home that he had hit the easiest ball of the match, OUT. He couldn't believe his eyes.

Surely he was mistaken, but there was the outstretched arm of the linesman indicating it was out. "How could I have done that?" agonised Jack. Various explanations rushed through his mind, "Maybe I tried to hit it too hard or maybe I shouldn't have tried to hit it so close to the line or maybe I got too excited?"

While all Jack's explanations may be true it is almost certain that once Jack saw that opening in the court and got excited he forgot to switch his attention back to the ball itself. Simply put, he didn't see the ball as he hit it.

The ability to have a thought about the shot you wish to play and return your attention to the ball is an art that needs practice.

ATTACHMENT CAN STIFLE CREATIVITY

Another problem with Jack's explanation of why he made his mistake could be that he becomes critical of himself for the wrong reasons. Misunderstanding the real reasons for his mistake may mean that he curbs his flair or creativity.

I've discovered that many players imagine a particular shot and when it doesn't come off criticize themselves for attempting it. They might tell themselves: "What a stupid shot to try and don't do it again."

This may be true, but another possibility is that they have become excited by the prospect of the shot they've imagined and in doing so have not shifted their attention back to the ball.

One of the greatest feelings in sport comes when we imagine something and it happens. It would be a shame to kill this pleasure for the wrong reasons. I can still recall the feeling of playing a particular shot in my mind's eye and looking up and seeing the actual shot following the imagined one as though it was sitting on the tail of a comet. All that separated them was the instant of time when I shifted my attention back to the ball.

Not all players are negatively influenced by the need to win. Some players use it as a spur for self-development. However, for others the need to win is possibly the greatest danger to their development. With a society that places great emphasis on the result, players are under enormous pressure to win. They may be tempted to hang on to a style or game that helps them win in the short term but has limitations for the future.

With the constant reinforcement of people asking, "Did you win? What was the score?", it becomes very difficult to take risks. Rarely would someone ask, "Did you take any new risks out there today?" or "I saw you try something different — that was terrific!"

With this in mind it is easy to see how a player about to play a shot, when suddenly faced with the thought, "If you miss this shot it will cost you the match," tightens up and probably doesn't see the ball at all. It becomes lost in the emotions surrounding that thought. When the need to win becomes too dominant the value of competition is lost.

I've found it interesting when coaching adults that frequently their games stop developing after a period of time. Quite often they set their sights on beating a certain person, and when they do beat that person they stop developing. Twenty years later their game has not changed. There is no spontaneity or creativity, no risks, no new shots. Their game is almost mechanical. Interest is completely centered around the result.

We should ask ourselves, "If we were learning a skill that didn't have win/lose at stake (let's say a language) how would we feel if we were no better after twenty-five years than we were after five?"

The short story, "The one that got away," demonstrates how our attachment to a particular outcome can change as our circumstances change.

The one that
got away

One day a fisherman untied his small boat and headed out to sea. He looked forward to the challenge of matching wits with the creatures of the deep. And of course there was always the lure of catching the big one.

Having cast his line, he settled down and waited. Knowing how to wait was part of the game. It wasn't long before there was a violent tug on the line. His adrenalin started to flow as he released the line, giving his opponent plenty of slack to play with. From the resistance, he knew that to win this battle would require all his experience and resources.

Time disappeared in the intense struggle. Stretched to his limit he felt that he might not be able to hold on, but he kept digging deeper, until unexpectedly he began to feel the fish weaken. With the prospect of winning the fight he felt a renewed surge of strength. He began to draw his trophy closer to the boat. Not far now. Peering into the water, the fisherman could see his prey only yards away. A sense of victory started to well up inside. "Wait till the others see what I bring in," he thought.

In that instant he relaxed and the fish sensing it was his last chance violently wrenched at the line and snapped it. The fisherman was stunned. So close and yet he'd lost.

Disappointed and exhausted, he started packing up trying to content himself with the prospect of telling his story about the one that got away.

Just as he was about to head back to shore he heard a terrific splash behind him. He turned and glimpsed the airborne marlin just before it knocked him into the sea. As the man landed in the water the fish traded places and landed with a thump in the boat. It was such a small boat the large creature almost totally filled it.

Stunned, the fisherman grabbed hold of the side of his vessel. Looking up, he could see the huge marlin in the boat staring back at him. He tried to climb back in but each time the fish lashed out so fiercely making it impossible. What was he to do? He stopped to think. "Don't panic," he told himself, "You'll be able to last longer in the water than the fish can in the boat. Just be patient and you'll be able to head back to shore with the prize after all. Not how you'd expected to win but this will make an even better story." Pleased with himself, he hung on and prepared to wait.

Now that the fisherman had stopped trying to climb into the boat, the fish stopped lashing out.

Time passed. "Not much longer," thought the man, when to his horror he looked up and saw a large fin heading in his direction. A shark!

The options passed quickly through his mind.

If he stayed in the water he would die and so would the fish. If the fish let him in the boat he would live and the fish could live as well. However, the fish had to trust him that he would let him go. On his past record that would be hard.

- What would you do if you were the fisherman?
- What would you do if you were the fish?

Dyeing the cloth

By now, it should be clear that one of the effects of competition is that it dredges up our beliefs about winning and losing. We have also discussed various methods for challenging inappropriate beliefs and how they affect our perception of the ball.

However, like any skill, if you practice the process of watching the ball consistently you will discover that the practice sessions will become similar to real competition.

A useful analogy for this process comes from the Indian tradition.

A guru was asked about the value of meditation in a busy life. He compared the process of meditation to the process of dyeing a cloth. In India when a piece of cloth is dyed it is dipped in the chosen color and hung in the sun to dry. Some of the color remains but some also fades. Once dry the cloth is again dipped into the color and once more hung out in the sun. Again some of the color fades, but this time it is a little darker than before. This process is continued until the dye becomes so embedded in the fabric that it barely fades when placed in the sun.

In the same way, the more you practice as though in competition, the more the process of watching the ball will stick. There will be less distinction between practice and match play.

WATCHING THE BALL IMPROVES TECHNIQUE

There are situations where watching the ball improves a player's technical skills.

An example of this could be when a player hits a backhand. One problem in playing a backhand is that the person about to play the shot releases the racket too sharply which causes their head to lift up quickly. This is often accompanied by the body weight being thrown onto the back foot and the ball being lifted out of court.

There are many instructions that could remedy this problem.

1. Release the racket smoothly. By releasing the racket this way, your head is less likely to jerk upwards, therefore resulting in better timing and a more rhythmical shot.

2. Keep the head still. By doing this, it is much more likely that you will actually see the ball. The only problem with this is that you can feel a little stiff and awkward keeping your head from moving.

3. Hold the weight over the front foot. By keeping the front foot firmly planted on the ground it may anchor your shot. It may help to keep your head from lifting and create a more balanced shot.

4. Watch the ball after the bounce.

If you watch the ball after the bounce your head can't go up in the air. If the head is kept down, the body weight usually stays balanced and we are compelled to release the racket in a more controlled manner.

I believe this is extremely useful because we need to see the ball anyway and so instead of complicating the moment of hitting with extra thoughts like "keeping the head still" and so on, we can keep the whole process simple.

Obviously if there are glaring technical problems they will need to be ironed out with the usual disciplined approach.

The more aspects of our game that we can program so that they are automatic, the greater our clarity for the parts that require conscious attention.

TIMING AND THE BALL

"What sort of things do you remember best?" Alice ventured to ask.

"Oh, things that happened the week after next," the Queen replied in a careless tone. "For instance, now," she went on, "there's the King's Messenger. He's in prison now being punished; and the trial doesn't even begin till next Wednesday; and of course the crime comes last of all."

In *The Way of Zen* Alan Watts writes of how the late Sokei-an Sasaki found *Alice in Wonderland* to be an admirable manual to express the point of view contained in some *koans*.

What is time and timing? Our ancestors measured the passage of time by observing cycles in Nature, Day and Night, Tides. Today physicists have precise instruments, such as atomic clocks, that are so reliable that it would take a million years for two such clocks to be out of synchrony by one second.

Yet it is interesting that the human perception of time can vary so dramatically. This relative experience of time is one of the theories for which Einstein is famous. In order to simplify the concept, Einstein devised the following simple, somewhat sexist, explanation for his secretary: "An hour sitting with a pretty girl passes like a minute; a minute sitting on a hot stove seems like an hour."

Today biologists and physicists are telling us that time is a concept that is influenced by our senses. Some days time seems to fly, other days it seems to drag, while at other times it appears to stand still. What is even more interesting is that physiologists are finding that our bodies are eavesdropping on the communication we are having with ourselves and our physiologies are responding to this conversation. As Dr Deepak Chopra (leading figure in mind/body medicine) says in his "Time and Immortality" lecture: "If our physiology hears our self-talk saying, 'there isn't time' or 'I'm running out of time' and there is a sense of urgency about our experience of time then our physiology responds by producing adrenalin, by increasing our heart rate, our blood pressure, etc."

One way to discover your inner dialog and how you experience time is to see how you respond to the time after the bounce of the ball. That is, do you feel rushed like the Rabbit in *Alice in Wonderland* who said, "No time to say Hello or Goodbye, I'm late, I'm late, I'm late"? Or do you feel there is plenty of time from the bounce to your racket? Of course this is in some ways dependent on the speed and placement of the ball that is being hit to you. However, if you keep observing this process each time you play you might begin to notice that a ball hit at the same speed from one session to another may appear, subjectively, to travel at different speeds.

I have noticed after experimenting with this process that the time from the bounce to my racket can feel very different. Often this is dependent on what has gone on before I stepped onto the court. I may feel as though I have all the time in the world, long enough for a cup of tea, or conversely, the time may seem to be full of urgency as though I were confronting a live hand grenade. The ball seems to be acting as a mirror, feeding back to me my mental and emotional state.

Try experimenting with this process. If you find that there seems very little time from the bounce onwards and the message from your brain is screaming urgently to hit it, see what happens if you can risk not listening to this voice and begin to hold onto the shot a little longer. It is interesting to note how many top sportspeople appear unhurried and at times almost casual.

Don't be frightened to experiment with your sense of time. The saying "having the ball on a string" has its basis in this idea. The ball can actually appear suspended on a string. There is often a timeless quality to this experience, as though we had a movie camera and were freeze framing the ball from instant to instant.

When time comes to a standstill so does the breath. Time and breath are the movement of thought and when thought comes to a standstill we have a *satori* or "peak experience."

These breathtaking moments are the ones where poetry, art and any inspiration comes from.

OPPONENT: UNPAID THERAPIST?

Having practiced the skill of watching the ball over a period of time, you may begin to notice that it is your opponent's task to try to hit a shot that actually disturbs your inner control and takes your attention from the ball. What they may do is to turn the volume up on your attitudes and fears. As discussed earlier, these fears have always been there, buried in your sub-conscious. But it wasn't until your opponent's shot unsettled you that they surfaced. In some ways they are is doing the job of a therapist, dredging and surfacing your self-limiting attitudes.

Again, this is where the ball is an invaluable aid. If you can keep looking for the ball it can become like a psychological anchor, a little like being thrown a rope when you're sliding into a crocodile pit of self-doubt and fear.

WHAT'S MUM OR DAD DOING AT THE OTHER END OF THE COURT?

If one of our parents has a very dominant personality and we have had difficulty in asserting ourselves with them we may find that this pattern repeats itself in sporting situations. We may be playing someone with a similarly strong or aggressive personality and feel overwhelmed by them. This inability to hold our ground will need to be remedied so that it doesn't continue to undermine our performances.

Another situation that causes some problems for young tennis players is when the parent's drive for their child to succeed is so strong that it may place more pressure on the child than they can handle. This may lead to resentment because the child feels that their self-esteem and their parent's affection is linked to whether they win or not.

Unless it is established clearly that the parent is supporting and encouraging the child regardless of the result then at some point in the child's life the problem of who they are playing for will surface. Are they playing in order to realize their parent's unfulfilled dreams or are they playing for their own sense of achievement and satisfaction?

I guess the message here for parents is that they need to walk that fine line between encouragement and interest in their child's development and being too driven or obsessive.

One useful process that can help resolve any of these inner dialog conflicts is to set up off the court a chance to hear these different inner voices. This is useful because it gives each person the opportunity to hear exactly what they are saying to themselves and to learn new responses when necessary.

WHEN IS A GREAT SHOT DANGEROUS?

Many players think it is only when they are playing badly that mistakes can happen. This is not true, however. How many times have you played a terrific point only to follow it up with a lousy one? How often do we see two terrific points, one after the other? Not often! What can happen after you have played and won a rally with an outstanding shot is that you feel so pleased with yourself you are still replaying the point in your mind when the next point begins. In hanging on to the euphoria of the last point you will be lucky if you see the next ball at all.

Again this is where the ritual and discipline of seeing every ball is so important.

TENNIS "RITUALS"

I've noticed in myself and in the people I coach that in the heat of competition we get a little more revved up than usual, and because of this we have a tendency to rush. At the time, this can be difficult to objectively assess, know or monitor. This is where it is important to have a set of in-built "rituals" that will help regulate our tempo on the court.

Two of the most important moments in tennis are those before we receive serve and those before we serve. These are ideal moments in which to self-monitor and check that our focus is in the appropriate place. They provide an opportunity to draw on Ball, Body and Breath.

The importance of ritual is something that has been known for thousands of years. It adds stability to our behavior and our actions and is a part of every culture.

SERVING

Before serving the ball it is useful to have a little checklist of thoughts. The ones I consider important are:

1. Decide where you are going to serve, that is backhand or forehand? Although this seems self-explanatory, over the years I've seen many players stand at the service line and crunch down their fastest, and best, serve straight to their opponent's strength. Remember that a well-placed serve is often better than pure brute strength.

2. Are you going into the net or are you staying back? On most occasions this decision needs to be made before you serve. If you serve and then decide you will often be caught out of position.

3. What sort of serve are you going to do? Are you going to use a powerful flat serve or topspin? Are you better off mixing up the serve so that your opponent doesn't get into a rhythm on return?

4. Relax hand on racket and take a deep breath. If you observe closely the serving hand of many of the top players you will notice that they relax their fingers on the grip before starting their service action. This allows for a relaxed smooth swing that maintains rhythm.

5. The last memory should always be "watch the ball." This is probably the most important point of all. For many players the service toss varies slightly and so if we swing automatically without a clear perception of the ball our timing may be off. Watching the ball means that this swing is timed to this ball.

Having a clear routine is necessary for two reasons. Firstly it is obvious that we need to make decisions regarding how we are going to play the point but just as important is that, by having the discipline of consciously checking what we are doing, this process acts as a stabilizing influence when we are under pressure and tempted to rush. If we religiously go through our checklist then for that time our attention is absorbed in what we need to do and taken away from any self-limiting or negative thoughts. The ritual therefore serves as an emotional anchor. By counting out the items and consciously answering the questions your attention is held where it needs to be, in the moment.

RECEIVING RITUALS

Before receiving serve we can again go through a checklist to try and prepare ourselves for the point ahead.

1. Relax grip and check breath is regular. Use this checkpoint to check that you are relaxed. It is interesting to note how relaxation and attachment to the result affect the return of serve. This is highlighted especially on the first serve. In many cases the first serve of a player is much faster than their second. How many times have you waited to return the first serve and it's a fault. It could even be very long and wayward but because it's a fault and doesn't matter we swing freely and hit what would have been a blinding winner. The second serve follows at half the pace, giving us plenty of time to see it and we play a dud shot into the net. Because of win/lose and fear of mistakes we tighten up and make mistakes.

2. Consciously see the ball toss of your opponent. This is the moment to check in. (It is easy to be focused on a thought without realizing it so it is useful to consciously see this ball so you are not suddenly woken up when the ball arrives.)

3. Remember to see the ball bounce before you hit it. Many people lose their perception of time when their senses pick up the fact the ball is coming quickly. They panic. Instead of using the time that's available they overreact and swing early. This leads to mis-timing the ball altogether.

Learning to respond appropriately can be difficult to master. A useful exercise to practice is to have someone serve fast to you. Initially be content to just stop the ball with your racket without worrying about trying to return it. Notice the time after the bounce. Once you feel that you can see it clearly start trying to return the ball while watching it.

If you are still feeling pressured you can create more time for yourself by moving further back in the court. As you become more confident with this process experiment with moving forward again. Have a little fun and see how far in you can stand and still see the ball. Remember this is a PRACTICE exercise.

Over the years I've found that many people actually have a tendency to swing early on a return of serve. It appears to be a difficult shot to wait for.

A final point about these moments before receiving serve and serving: Always wait until you are ready to play the point before you start. It is important to establish your own presence on the court. If an opposition player can rush you and pressure you to play the match at their tempo you may feel as though you are unable to settle into your own rhythm.

Recently I participated in a public speaking course and it became quite noticeable to each of us how difficult it is to hold the audience's attention at the beginning of a speech. Our nervous tension pushed us into starting our talk before we were really ready.

One night we spent time practicing waiting at the podium before we spoke. Initially it was difficult to hang on until we had the audience's attention but once we gained a little confidence it became clear how powerful this moment could be.

In much the same way it is easy to step up to the line to serve and be driven by the extra adrenalin of the moment. So practice containing this urgency so that you establish early in the match that you are PRESENT.

PLAYING WITH THE
GRAPHIC EQUALIZER

Having spent some time familiarizing yourself with
the previous chapters, it is important to decide, at any
particular practice session, where your emphasis needs
to lie. Do you need to watch the ball more closely
after the bounce? Do you need to spend more time
relaxing and monitoring your grip? And so on. For
instance, you may feel that you are focused on the ball
and seeing it clearly after the bounce, and yet you may
not feel that you are hitting the ball well. If that's the
case then you may need to spend more time on
relaxing your hand. In the end you might see yourself
playing with the dials of your stereo turning up the
base or treble until you get the tuning you want. This
fine tuning might be slightly different each time or
you may begin to notice that you need to work on
one particular area more than others.

This ball

Each Point, Game
Set and Match slips by
All unnoticed

Players
Absorbed, preoccupied
Or lost
In the same safe
But deadening patterns
Until
Mysteriously
A light illumines
This moment,
This shot, this ball
Apparently new

Ah Ha!!
The watcher becomes
Aware of itself
And realizes
Where the mind goes
There the eye follows

This the player sees.

EPILOG

A TENNIS *SESSHIN*

Early in my tennis coaching days I was tempted to give too much instruction. Each pupil seemed hungry for information and it was tempting to give them a detailed account of everything in their game that required change.

Unfortunately, while that made me appear very knowledgeable, it rarely led to good results. Many times the pupil who had left in an optimistic frame of mind, armed with a mental recipe book for solving any tennis problem, would return the next week frustrated and despondent at how their game had actually got worse, not better.

In time I learnt to hold back information until they were ready to take in more. Managing change in their game meant striking a balance between getting rid of the old, creating the new and maintaining some stability in the process. By doing this they could make sustainable progress.

However, for those who are extremely enthusiastic about getting on with things I would suggest they try to create more time for a concentrated approach.

Sustainable change either needs to be gradual or requires a concentrated effort to bring it about.

If your game has reached a plateau or you're keen to break new ground, I would encourage you try a tennis *sesshin* in order to make smoother and quicker transitions in your game. In the Zen tradition *sesshins* (intensives) are designed to give practitioners the opportunity to gain deeper insights into their practice.

The word *sesshin* actually means to unite the mind. During these *sesshins*, monks or keen practitioners of Zen would do more intensive periods of meditation, chanting and ceremony.

A tennis *sesshin* gives you a chance to practice and combine the techniques discussed in this book and hopefully gain a glimpse of your game at a higher level.

PLANNING YOUR
TENNIS SESSHIN

It's important before you start your intensive that you have planned each detail so that you don't find yourself having to make too many decisions during it.

How long?

The first decision to make is how long and how intense an experience you want. The Zen *sesshins* often last for seven days. The days are structured from early morning to night.

How much time are you going to allot to your intensive? Have you a whole day, a weekend or a week?

Who with?

It would be ideal to have a group of like-minded people involved in the *sesshin*. There is strength in numbers. Obviously, as this is a tennis intensive, it will help if your hitting partners are at a similar level. However, as long as each person in the group has someone of comparable ability to hit with it won't matter if there are varying standards within the group. Obviously for the meditation, meals and walking components, tennis ability is irrelevant.

Whereabouts?

Once you have been able to organize a group, work out where the *sesshin* will take place. Which tennis courts? Could you go into the country and make it a retreat?

Food

Preparation and acquisition of the food needs to be considered beforehand so that the routine is not interrupted. Having gone to the trouble of organizing this time try to make the food nutritious and enjoyable.

Due to the high exercise component of the day it is important to have a high intake of complex carbohydrates. These foods include whole grains, fruit, breads, vegetables, pastas and potatoes. This will provide the necessary fuel for the day's activities.

Which meditation activities?

Two important ones discussed are:

1. Mantra meditation, which is useful for clearing the mind and is a similar process to watching the ball.

2. Progressive relaxation can help you gain some body awareness and relaxation to take onto the court.

Throughout the book we have looked at various exercises designed to create a greater awareness of our attitudes, thoughts, body and breath. Which of these exercises appeal to you? You may wish to practice one technique for the complete length of your intensive or you may wish to experiment with a range.

Which tennis activities?

When planning this aspect, consider some of the activities discussed in the book. Some of these are:

- Watching the ball (see page 137).

- Monitoring tension (see page 77).

- Putting it all together, for example the serving and receiving exercises (see pages 145–48).

○

TENNIS *SESSHIN*

Stick to your timetable or else you'll end up chopping and changing times too much. Once you've decided on your routine it's valuable to slot yourself into it with as little fuss as possible.

6.00 a.m.

Early start. In a Zen *sesshin* a typical day might begin at 4.45 a.m. This would probably be a shock to most of us, so let's try for a 6 a.m. rising. Take half an hour to wash and wake up.

6.30 a.m.

Either individually or as a group do some light stretching or have a half-hour walk. At this time in a Zen *sesshin* the participants would be in the midst of a two-and-a-half-hour *Zazen/kinhin* meditation. Make this very easy and gentle. It is a slow wake-up for the body, not an aerobic activity.

7.00 a.m.

This is meditation time. Which of the exercises have you chosen? Some of the possibilities are:

- *Zazen* meditation (page 114)

- visualization exercise (page 100)

- progressive relaxation (page 91).

You might want to use a combination. Decide this in your planning session before the intensive begins.

8.00 a.m.

Breakfast. Try to make it healthy. Typical breakfast foods would be whole grain cereals (muesli), fruit, toast and high fiber wholemeal muffins. Make sure that you drink water regularly throughout the morning, especially in warm conditions.

9.00 a.m.

Tennis practice — 90 minutes

Warm up slowly. It is useful before you even hit a ball to do some Tai Chi tennis and slowly swing through a tennis routine. Focus on the feeling of your strokes flowing effortlessly. Now that your body is warm start with slow relaxed hitting. You could follow the Six-stage Hitting Plan and start by watching the ball as in Step 1. See how the time after the bounce feels. Do you feel urgent or relaxed. Then add the movement of Step 2. Feel yourself moving effortlessly around the court, following the flight and bounce of the ball.

The last half hour of this time could be used for practicing serving and receiving rituals.

10.30 a.m.

Morning tea break — 30 minutes

During this break you could talk over with your practice partner your experience of the morning. This could be a useful time to make a few notes as to other ideas, thoughts for future practice times.

Fruit juice or easily digestible fruit like bananas would help keep the blood sugar levels up.

11.00 a.m.

Tennis practice — 90 minutes

If you felt comfortable with the processes in the earlier session then you could move on to using the next steps of the Six-stage Hitting Plan. This involves playing points. At first play points without worrying about the score. See if you hold your focus for the ball. You might check that you relax your hand on the racket between shots. Then move into scoring. Again observe whether you can maintain the same focus and relaxation.

The last half hour could revolve around staying relaxed and focused at the net. Stay on your toes, keep your hands relaxed and look for the ball. Obviously, you will have less time to see the ball when you are at the net. This exercise is often done in short bursts.

In a Zen *sesshin* this part of the morning could be filled with more *Zazen* mediation, chanting or a talk.

12.30 p.m.

Lunch

Low fat, high carbohydrate meals for lunch could include sandwiches, salads, fruit or dried fruits. Control the amount you eat because you will be running around in less than an hour. Remember to drink a couple of glasses of water.

2.00 p.m.

Tennis practice — 2 hours

Start with a warm up. Then if you have been happy with your progress this morning you could move into playing matches with normal tennis scoring. Again notice how you respond to the pressure. Can you maintain your attention for the ball and feel relaxed at the same time.

Leave fifteen minutes at the end to warm down. You could go back to light hitting or you could do some light stretching.

4.00 p.m.

30 minute break

Having finished tennis for the day it would probably be useful to use this time to freshen up. Have a shower and change into some light comfortable clothes ready for your afternoon meditation session.

4.30 p.m.

Meditation — 1 hour

Use the mediation technique you have chosen.

You may wish at this stage to repeat the meditation technique you used this morning or you might like to try something different. If you had difficulty with an aspect of your game during the day, using the visualization, Meet the Inner Coach, might be useful.

5.30 p.m.

Free time — 1 hour

This could be a valuable time to fill out your journal to bring to the evening session. Write a short overview of the day. How was the experience of meditation? Could you hold your focus on the tennis court?

6.30 p.m.

Dinner

The evening meal could consist of more complex carbohydrates such as pasta, vegetables, rice, potato, lentils and fruit salad. If your intensive is going for more than one day this meal will provide some of the fuel for tomorrow's activities.

7.30 p.m.

Use this time for a group meeting. How are you feeling by this stage of the day? Tired? Relaxed? Did anyone have a breakthrough? Did anyone gain any new insights into their game? Are there similarities between your responses to pressure on the court and your responses in other areas? If it is only a one-day *sesshin*, what aspect of your game could you focus on when you return to your club? You could use this time to fill out the dream/goal sheet or the *satori* sheet and use these for discussion.

10.00 p.m.

Lights out

During each day of the *sesshin* you have five hours of exercise blended with two hours of meditation. These times will draw on both physical and mental stamina. Being well rested is important.

This concentrated time provided by a tennis *sesshin* will give you the opportunity to put into practice the processes and techniques described in this book so that you experience:

- the possibility that tennis can be used as a vehicle for uncovering and transforming unconscious attitudes

- the value of being fully focused in the moment

- your true potential as a tennis player

- the connections between your philosophy of tennis and your philosophy of life

- the experience of *satori*.

The art of tennis

A splash of color
Bursts from the player's racket
An artist's brush
On a rectangular canvas

The ball
Leaving its mark
The circular dots
Of Aboriginal art

Feet tracing movements of
A modern ballet
Choreographed by the invisible strings
Of opposing shots

With clenched fists
Raised in victory and despair
Actors impassioned cries
Echo through the arena

This theater
of joy and sorrow
Enacting the tragedies and triumphs
Of the human spirit